I.

Revise for Edexcel GCSE Graphic Products

John Halliwell

Series Editor: Chris Weaving

Heinemann Educational Publishers
Halley Court, Jordan Hill, Oxford OX2 8EJ
Part of Harcourt Education Limited

Heinemann is the registered trademark of Harcourt Education Limited

© John Halliwell and Chris Weaving, 2003

First published 2003

07   06   05   04   03
10   9   8   7   6   5   4   3   2   1

British Library Cataloguing in Publication Data is available from the British Library on request.

ISBN 0 435 41721 5

Designed and typeset by Techset, Tyne and Wear

Original illustrations © Harcourt Education Limited, 2003

Illustrated by Techset, Tyne and Wear

Printed in the UK by The Bath Press Ltd

Cover photo: © Image Bank (top), Haddon Davies (middle), John Birdsall (bottom)

Acknowledgements
Every effort has been made to contact copyright holders of material reproduced in this book. Any omissions will be rectified in subsequent printings if notice is given to the publishers.

Tel: 01865 888058 email: info.he@heinemann.co.uk

CONTENTS

If yes read on …

What is revision?

Revision in preparation for an examination is defined as *reviewing previously learned material*.

Why revise?

The purpose of revision is to:
- *refresh your knowledge and understanding* of previously learned material;
- *improve your ability to recall and apply this knowledge and understanding* to the questions on the examination paper.

How can revision improve my grade?

The written examination paper:
- is worth 40% of the whole examination (the other 60% comes from coursework);
- has four questions, each worth 10% of the whole examination.

Therefore, thorough revision that enables four questions to be answered well, can earn a large proportion of these marks and contribute significantly to the final grade awarded.

Do I need to know about all the content listed in the Exam Board Specification?

Yes because:
- the examination board will test all content listed in the Specification at least once during its life (normally five years);
- if something has been tested once, it does not mean it will not be tested again in a future exam paper.

It is therefore essential that you prepare fully by revising everything listed in the Specification.

How does this book help me?

It has been written by examiners who know:
- how the questions are written;
- what is needed in the answers.

What does the book tell me?

The book contains important information about the examination paper and about what you need to know.

1 Section 1 tells you about the examination paper:
- how it is structured;
- how part questions are structured;
- the importance of *Key Words* in each part question;
- how to manage your time answering the questions;
- how to write your answers to access all of the marks.

2 Section 2 and Section 3:
- combine some content headings from the Examination Board Specification to form single *Topic* headings;
- show how these content headings must be integrated when applied to designing;
- help you to understand how to apply the knowledge and understanding you already have, to designing;
- help you focus your revision and make more effective use of that time.

3 Section 4 helps you to:
- understand the *Design Question* (not Short Course);
- understand the *Product Analysis Question*.
- recognise the types of part questions that may be included;
- recognise what is needed to answer each question successfully by giving sample answers.

Do the *Topics* tell me what I need to know to answer the exam questions?

Yes. These *Topics*:
- are introduced by identifying the major areas of the Specification content for which you need to have an appropriate level of knowledge and understanding;
- expand this content into *Key Points*.

What do the *Key Points* tell me?

The *Key Points*:
- identify the detail of what you need to know;
- focus the detail towards its application in product design and make/manufacture i.e. how different materials properties present design opportunities and how different making/manufacturing processes present design opportunities.

What about industrial applications?

The industrial applications icon will show where industrial processes are addressed within each *Topic*.

Are there any sample questions and answers?

Yes. Each *Topic* will include sample part questions, complete with full answers to show:
- how questions might be asked;
- the depth and breadth of knowledge and understanding required;
- how to present answers to access all of the marks.

 This icon indicates an Industrial Application

 This icon indicates information not required for the Short Course

Section 1: Revision strategy and explanation

THE QUESTION PAPER

Short course (SC)

There will be two different question papers, one each for the foundation and higher tiers. For the examination you will be given one of these papers.

The question paper will be marked out of a total of 44 marks.

The time for answering the paper is 1 hour.

All questions are compulsory and must be answered in the spaces provided on the question paper.

Each question paper will have three separate questions as follows:

- Two questions will test specific knowledge and understanding from AO1* and will be worth 11 marks each (see further guidance in this section and Section 2).

- One question will test product analysis AO3* (iii) and will be worth 22 marks (see Sections 3 and 4).

* AO1 and AO3 are the Assessment Objectives listed in Edexcel's Subject Specification booklet. They contain the knowledge and understanding that the examination questions will be based upon. Section 2 of this book deals with AO1 and Section 3 deals with AO3.

Examiner's Tip

To score as many marks as you are able, you must attempt all questions and part questions.

Full course (FC)

There will be two different question papers, one each for the foundation and higher tiers. For the examination you will be given one of these papers.

The question paper will be marked out of a total of 88 marks.

The time for answering the paper is $1\frac{1}{2}$ hours.

All questions are compulsory and must be answered in the spaces provided on the question paper.

Each question paper will have four separate questions as follows:

- One question, 22 marks, will test specific knowledge and understanding from AO1* (see further guidance in this section and Section 2).

- The first half of another question, 11 marks, will test different specific knowledge and understanding from AO1*, with the second half testing specific knowledge and understanding from AO3* (i) and (ii), 11 marks (see further guidance in this section and Sections 2 and 3).

- The design question, 22 marks, will test AO2* (see Section 4).
- The product analysis question, 22 marks, will test AO3 (iii) (see Section 4).

* AO1, AO2 and AO3 are the Assessment Objectives listed in Edexcel's Subject Specification booklet. AO1 and AO3 contain the knowledge and understanding that the examination questions will be based upon. Section 2 of this book deals with AO1 and Section 3 deals with AO3.

 xaminer's Tip

To score as many marks as you are able, you must attempt all questions and part questions.

Short course and Full course (SC/FC)

Each separate question will be divided into smaller part questions labelled (a), (b), (c), etc. These part questions are likely to be progressively more difficult.

Alphabetically labelled part questions, for example (a), may also be divided further into smaller parts and these are labelled (i), (ii), (iii), etc. These smaller parts will all be linked to the common theme of this part question.

The marks available for each part question are shown at the end of that part question, for example **(2 marks)**.

 xaminer's Tip

These marks also suggest how long you should spend answering each question, for example you should spend approximately twice as long thinking about and answering a question worth 2 marks compared to answering a question worth 1 mark.

On all question papers the potentially easier questions will be towards the beginning of the paper, with those that are potentially more difficult towards the end. This also applies to the part questions within a whole question, that is, there is an increase in difficulty between the beginning and end of the paper and between the beginning and end of each question.

 xaminer's Tip

Make sure each answer fully satisfies the question set, that is, if you give simple one-word answers to the more valuable questions, you will not score many marks.

How you should answer individual questions

Each part question will use a key word to tell you the type of answer that is required. The key words and answer types are as follows:

Key words	Answer type
Give State Name	Normally a one- or two-word answer, at the very most a short sentence.
Name the specific	As above, but requires specific detail to be given. Generic answers such as 'card' or 'plastic' will gain no marks.
Describe	Normally, one or two sentences which form a description, making reference to more than one point. All points must be linked for a complete answer.
Explain	Normally, one or two sentences which form an explanation. This requires a clear or detailed account of something and includes a relevant justification, reason or example.
Use notes and sketches Annotated sketches	Mainly a sketched answer with notes to support or clarify particular points in the answer. 'Sketch' means 'a quick freehand drawing'. Marks are awarded for the technical accuracy of the information communicated in the answer rather than the drawing skills shown.
Evaluate	Normally one or two sentences where the quality, suitability or value of something is judged. This can include both positive and negative points, with each point normally requiring a relevant justification, reason or example.

 xaminer's Tip

The number of pieces of information required in any answer will be shown by the number of marks given to the part question.

 xaminer's Tip

The space given on the question paper suggests the maximum that you should write or draw in answer to any question.

Examiner's Tip

No marks are given for repeating information given in the question.

Examiner's Tip

Where / is used in an example answer, it means that what follows is an alternative to the part of the answer that precedes it, not an addition.

The following example questions and answers illustrate the use of the main key words in part questions and the different style and length of answers required.

Q1 *Give **two** safety procedures which must be followed when using a hot melt glue gun.*

1 ....

2 .... **(2 marks)**

A full answer requires two different safety procedures to be stated, for example:

1 Keep fingers away from hot surfaces.

2 Return to its stand when not in use.

Q2 *20,000 copies of a promotional leaflet are to be printed using the lithographic printing processs. Describe **one** advantage of using lithography for this volume of production.*

....

.... **(2 marks)**

A full answer for 2 marks requires a statement containing two linked points, as shown below in **bold text**, for example:

Lithography produces **a good quality printed image** very **cost effectively**.

Q3 *A colour leaflet promoting the facilities available at a leisure centre is to be printed and distributed in its local area.*

(i) *Explain **two** reasons for having a gloss finish to the paper.*

1 ....

.... **(2 marks)**

2 ....

.... **(2 marks)**

A full answer for 4 marks requires two different reasons to be identified and the importance of each to be explained or justified, for example:

1 A **high quality finish** is required because **visual impact** is necessary.

2 The leaflet must be **durable** because users may wish to **keep it for reference for several months**.

Ⓔxaminer's Tip

Note that both of these answers have two parts to them, each linked by the word 'because'.

Section 2: Assessment Objective 1

GRAPHIC MEDIA

You need to know about:

☐ the range of tools and equipment available to the designer.

KEY POINTS

The term graphic media refers to tools and materials used by the product designer. These tools range from simple drawing equipment to sophisticated software applications. Computers are used increasingly, performing tasks which used to be carried out by hand.

Some of this equipment is generally available whereas some is specially designed to meet the needs of the designer. Many are used to produce formal, technical drawings such as:

• orthographic drawings • isometric drawings • perspective drawings.

 xaminer's Tip

You should be able to understand these drawing styles but you will not be tested on them in the exam.

Uses of graphic media

Equipment	Use
Pencils	Hard pencils (H to 9H) produce a lighter and more precise line. Used for detailed technical drawings, for example, where accuracy is important Soft pencils (HB to 9B) produce a darker and wider line. Used for sketching and shading Coloured pencils vary in quality. More expensive brands are softer and available in a wider range of colours
Fine liner pens	Fine liner pens can produce a clean even line when used properly Used for sketching, 'inking in' technical drawings and adding labels or notes to design sheets
Markers	Available as: • spirit or water based • chisel, bullet or brush point Spirit-based markers are quick drying and produce a more even finish but can be very expensive Used to add colour to large areas quickly. Used on presentation drawings to communicate the final look of a product design

Equipment	Use
Drawing boards	Used to produce technical drawings Parallel motions or tee squares are used in combination with other equipment to draw lines A3 is the most common size of board used in school but professionals use much larger boards
Set squares	A draughting aid to help draw lines at set angles The 60-degree set square is used for isometric work
Plastic rule	Used as a straight edge to draw lines Used as a measuring tool All dimensions should be given in millimetres
Compasses	Used to draw circles and arcs (parts of circles) More expensive examples such as bow compasses incorporate springs, adjustment mechanisms and can be used with a range of attachments
Eraser	Used to remove unwanted lines Better quality erasers do not smudge
Templates and stencils	Used as a guide to draw common shapes
French curves	Usually available in sets of three and used to draw a wide range of curves
Flexi-curves	Plastic strips filled with lead which can be bent to form any curve
Computer software applications	CAD packages (computer-aided design) – used to produce designs directly onto the computer DTP packages (desktop publishing) – used to design layouts for publications such as magazines and leaflets Draw packages – used to produce drawings, illustrations and diagrams Paint packages – used to produce coloured drawings, illustrations and diagrams
Photocopier	Black and white copiers reproduce and enlarge or reduce images and documents quickly and inexpensively Colour copiers are slower and much more expensive
Airbrush	Airbrushes will cover large and small areas with colour Ideal for representing surface finishes in presentation drawings because it is possible to blend colours Require skill and practice in order to achieve professional looking results

Examination questions

Q1 *Name the equipment pictured below and give an example of use for each.*

8 marks

a

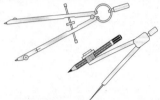

b

c

d

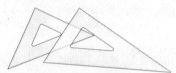

Acceptable answer

a Compasses – used to draw circles

b Airbrush – used to spray inks

c French curves – used to draw curves

d Set squares – used to draw lines at 90 degrees

xaminer's Tip

'Name' and 'Give' require a one- or two-word answer, or a short sentence at the most.

Q2 *Describe the difference between the type of line produced by hard and soft pencils with reference to their use.*

4 marks

Acceptable answer

Hard pencils (H to 9H): produce a **clean, sharp line**, which is more suitable for **draughting detailed technical drawings**.

Soft pencils (HB to 9B): produce a **dark, thick line** which is more suitable for **sketching and shading**.

xaminer's Tip

Two marks are awarded for correctly describing each type of line. Two marks are awarded for correctly describing the uses of each type

You need to know about:

□ the difference between aesthetics and function

□ the aesthetic properties of materials and components

□ the functional properties of materials and components

□ the working characteristics of materials and components

□ the general properties of modelling materials and commercial packaging materials.

KEY POINTS

In order to develop successful products designers have to make decisions when selecting materials and components based upon their individual **functional properties**, **aesthetic properties** and **working characteristics**. They need to be sure that they have chosen the material or component which will do the best job.

AESTHETICS AND FUNCTION

The term **aesthetics** in relation to materials, components or products refers to the qualities which make them look attractive.

The **function** of a material, component or product refers to the work that it is supposed to carry out, in other words, the purpose of that material, component or product.

It is the task of the designer to design products which are both visually appealing and which work effectively.

AESTHETIC PROPERTIES

Visual Impact

The ability of a material or component to attract our attention is described as its visual impact. This depends on:

• shape   • colour   • form (3D shape)   • surface finish   • pattern   • texture.

For example, paper with a marbled pattern is often used for certificates to enhance their visual appeal.

Colour

Materials and components are selected because of their natural colour or because they will accept an appropriate finish such as enamel spray paint. For example, acrylic is often chosen to make signs because it is available in a wide range of bright colours requiring little finishing.

Colours are associated with qualities and feelings. Designers use this by selecting colours which suit the product. If you specify a colour in one of your designs, you should be able to justify your choice in your general annotation.

Colour association

Colour	Associations	Uses
Greens	Safety, environmentally friendly, growth, nature, freshness, lime flavours, cleanliness	Environmentally friendly product packaging Cleaning products

When it is important to specify exact colour, designers use systems such as the Pantone index which describes every hue and tone as a number.

Surface Finish

Surface finish is added to materials to improve:

- aesthetic/visual properties
- functional/physical properties.

Materials are available in a range of surface finishes. Some materials can be moulded or polished while others can be combined with other materials through coating or lamination processes. For example, posters can be laminated with plastic to give a higher quality, glossy feel which allows the poster to be cleaned easily and to last longer.

Texture

Materials and components are available in a range of textures. In addition, texture can be added to materials to improve the appeal of a product through manufacturing processes such as moulding and embossing or by adding other materials. For example, a foam model for a new camera design can be enhanced by adding small, self-adhesive, paper circles which can be sprayed. When a casing for a working camera is manufactured, texture is achieved through the injection moulding process.

FUNCTIONAL PROPERTIES

Durability

Some materials and components last much longer than others and will stand up to much more wear and tear. This is known as durability. For example, polythene plastic bags used for shopping will last longer and resist wear more effectively than paper bags.

Strength

Materials and components have different strengths. Strength is the ability of a material to withstand forces without breaking. For example, plastics are much stronger than glass, which is very fragile. As a result, plastic bottles can be made much lighter than their glass counterparts.

Thickness

Materials vary in thickness. For example, cardboards are available in a wide range of thicknesses measured in microns. Thicker boards are heavier but stronger than thinner boards.

Rigidity

The term rigidity refers to the ability to resist bending. A rigid material will be stiff, the opposite to flexible. For example, Low Density Polythene displays low rigidity and is very flexible. It makes good 'squeegee' bottles which are needed to dispense thick liquids such as shampoos and washing-up liquids.

Special machinery is available to test the functional properties of materials and products.

WORKING CHARACTERISTICS OF MATERIALS AND COMPONENTS

These refer to the way in which a material or component behaves when it is used to make things. For example, polystyrene foam cuts very easily using a range of tools and can be sanded to a very smooth finish; polythene can be 'melted' and reformed which makes it suitable for the injection moulding process.

PROPERTIES OF MODELLING MATERIALS

The reasons for selecting modelling materials include:

- working properties which make them easy to cut and shape
- rigidity or flexibility
- suitability for desired finish
- cost.

PROPERTIES OF COMMERCIAL PACKAGING MATERIALS

The reasons for selecting commercial packaging materials include:

- strength
- durability
- rigidity or flexibility
- weight
- suitability for printing
- suitability for manufacturing processes
- aesthetic qualities such as colour or transparency
- cost
- suitability for recycling
- impermeability to germs, gases, liquids and/or light
- ability to withstand temperatures
- impact resistance
- puncture resistance.

Examination questions

 *When developing packaging designs for a new fizzy drink product the designers have recommended the use of PET. Give **two** properties of PET which make it a suitable material for a fizzy drinks bottle.*

Acceptable answer
PET is completely **transparent** and is **durable**.

Examiner's Tip
'Give' requires a one- or two-word answer, or a short sentence at the most.

 *Describe **one** property of Expanded Polystyrene Foam which makes it a suitable choice of material for making three-dimensional models.*

Acceptable answer
Expanded Polystyrene Foam can be **sanded very smooth**, and once sealed **can be sprayed to produce a high quality finish**.

Examiner's Tip
'Describe' requires one or two sentences referring to at least two points which are linked.

You need to know about:

- ☐ the common properties and working characteristics of papers and boards
- ☐ the properties, working characteristics and applications of individual paper and boards.

KEY POINTS

There are hundreds of different types of paper and boards to choose from. They are used extensively by the designer for modelling and as commercial packaging materials. The properties and working characteristics of papers and boards can be categorised by their:

- size
- weight or thickness
- colour
- surface finish and texture

- cost
- ability to accept graphic media
- ability to be cut, shaped and formed.

SIZE

Paper and boards are usually supplied in standard sizes. Commercial papers and thin cards are also available on rolls which are used in continuous 'web-fed' processes such as the lithographic printing process used to produce newspapers.

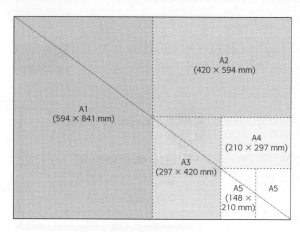

Common 'A' sizes of paper

WEIGHT AND THICKNESS

Papers and boards are usually described in terms of:

- weight (gsm – grams per square metre), or
- thickness (microns – short for micrometres).

Paper becomes a board after approximately 220 microns.

COLOUR

Colour can be added:

- as a dye during manufacture
- as a thin surface layer
- through printing.

SURFACE FINISH AND TEXTURE

There are many surface finishes available:

- Coated papers are coated to improve smoothness and quality.
- Laminated papers and boards allow layers of a higher quality material to be added to improve surface quality.

COST

Cost depends on the quality and quantity of the paper or board required. Specialist boards such as mounting board can be very expensive. Recycled papers and boards tend to be cheaper.

ABILITY TO ACCEPT GRAPHIC MEDIA

Papers and boards are often designed for specific purposes. For example:

- Fine liner pens used on tracing paper produce a very clean and sharp line.
- Copier paper is purpose designed to produce high quality prints from photocopiers but is also a very good general purpose, sketching and writing paper.

ABILITY TO BE CUT, SHAPED, FORMED AND JOINED

Paper and card can be shaped, formed and joined by:

- cutting
- scoring/creasing and folding
- moulding (e.g. egg cartons)
- pinning and stapling
- binding (e.g. comb binder)
- gluing.

The properties, working characteristics and applications of individual paper and boards

Paper	Significant properties	Uses	Advantages
Layout paper	50 gsm Very thin Translucent Smooth Off white in colour Relatively expensive	Outline sketches of page layouts Sketching and developing ideas	Translucency allows tracing Usually bleed proof making it ideal for spirit markers
Tracing paper	60/90 gsm Thin Almost transparent Very smooth Pale grey in colour Expensive, especially when using heavier weights	Outline sketches of page layouts Sketching and developing ideas Accurate working drawings Heavier weights preferred by draughtsmen	Transparency allows tracing and overlaying of designs Smooth surface finish allows designer to produce very fine lines when using ink pens
Copier paper	80 gsm Lightweight Smooth Bright white or coloured Inexpensive	Black and white photocopying and printing General classroom use for sketching and writing	Good, cheap, general purpose paper available in bright white or a range of colours

Paper	Significant properties	Uses	Advantages
Cartridge paper	120–150 gsm Available in heavier weights Fine textured surface Creamy white in colour Completely opaque Relatively inexpensive but depends upon weight and quality	General purpose drawing and painting paper	Heavier weights are suitable for use with paint Versatile
Grid paper	80 gsm Printed with feint grid pattern Available in squared or isometric	Guide lines are used to construct graphs, charts or 3D shapes	Reduces the need for drawing equipment

Board	Significant properties	Uses	Advantages
Mounting board	1000–1500 microns Very thick High quality Smooth or textured colour layer applied to one surface Very expensive	Presentation of work either as a supporting surface or as a frame	Strong, rigid Available in a wide range of colours High quality finish
Solid board and card (including boards used for commercial packaging)	220–750 microns A variety of boards available in a range of thicknesses, colour, surface finish/texture and quality Commercial boards are often built up from two or more layers of differing quality to reduce costs Relatively expensive when compared with paper but depends upon weight, finish and quality	Thinner card can be used in photocopiers and printers 3D modelling Packaging mock-ups Presentation of work Most forms of packaging including boxes and cartons	Available in a large range of colours and finishes Strong Rigid Can be scored, creased or bent Can be coated or laminated to improve quality or performance Can be produced with excellent printing surface
Corrugated card (including corrugated board used for commercial packaging)	Fluted paper sandwiched between paper layers (liners) available in single, double and triple wall boards. More layers produce stronger materials Flutes vary in size: larger flutes result in stronger material finer, smaller flutes produce better printing surface Low cost	Protective packaging for fragile products, e.g. large 'brown' cardboard boxes containing electrical goods Thinner corrugated card with finer flutes used to package high quality products such as perfume bottles	Excellent impact, puncture and tear resistance and durability Excellent stacking strength Excellent strength to weight ratio (lightweight) Cost can be reduced by using recycled materials High quality papers such as Kraft papers with excellent print surfaces can be used for outer layers

single wall

double wall

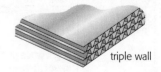

triple wall

Corrugated cards

Examination questions

Q1 *Explain **two** reasons why designers prefer to use layout paper when developing their ideas.*

4 marks

Acceptable answer

1 Layout paper is **translucent** because designers like to **trace previous designs** as they develop their ideas.

2 Layout paper is normally **bleed proof** because this allows designers to **use spirit markers accurately**.

xaminer's Tip

'Explain' requires you to justify your answer. Make sure you use words like 'because'. You will be awarded 2 marks for correctly identifying two properties of layout paper and 2 marks for explaining why these properties make the material a suitable choice.

Q2 *Give the metric unit used to measure the weight of paper.*

1 mark

Acceptable answer

Grams per square metre.

PLASTICS

TOPICS

You need to know about:

☐ the common properties and working characteristics of plastics

☐ the properties, working characteristics and applications of individual plastics as modelling and commercial packaging materials.

KEY POINTS

Plastics are divided into two groups:

- Thermoplastics can be reformed by applying heat.
- Thermoset plastics once 'set' cannot be reformed.

PROPERTIES AND WORKING CHARACTERISTICS OF PLASTICS

Packaging is produced almost exclusively from thermoplastics.

Most plastics display many common properties. Below are the main reasons why plastics are used in packaging:

- versatile
- lightweight
- low cost
- energy saving
- tough and durable
- recyclable
- impact resistant
- most can be made translucent or transparent
- available in a range of colours
- available in a range of forms (e.g. sheets, tubes, granules)
- water-resistant
- can be thermoformed (shaped using heat)
- can be printed.

Many plastics can be used for similar purposes. Both LDPE and PVC are used to make cling film, for example. In addition, adding other chemicals can change the properties of plastics.

Plastics can be shaped, formed and joined by:

- cutting
- drilling
- moulding
- welding
- gluing.

The properties, working characteristics and applications of individual plastics

Material	Significant properties	Uses	Advantages
PET Polyethylene Terephthalate (Commercial packaging material)	Excellent transparency Very tough Impenetrable to gases Can withstand a wide range of temperatures	Fizzy drink bottles Food containers Microwaveable food trays	Glass-like transparency allows product to be seen Does not affect flavour of food products Ideal for use as packaging for oven-ready/microwaveable products
HDPE High Density Polythene (Commercial packaging material)	Excellent chemical resistance Good barrier to water	Bottles and containers, e.g. for: • washing-up liquid • cosmetics Thin sheet packaging	Very suitable for containers designed to hold a wide range of liquids and which need to be tough, durable and flexible Very common form of packaging
PVC Polyvinyl Chloride (Commercial packaging material)	Rigid – can be flexible if plasticisers are added Excellent chemical resistance Good barrier to weather/water/gases	Shrink wrapping and cling film Blister packaging Packaging for: • toiletries • pharmaceuticals products • food • confectionery • water • fruit juices	Very versatile, can be used for a wide variety of products Chemical resistance makes rigid PVC suitable for products such as batteries or pharmaceutical products (drugs and medicines)

Plastics

20

Material	Significant properties	Uses	Advantages
LDPE Low Density Polythene (Commercial packaging material)	Soft, flexible Excellent chemical resistance Good barrier to water but not gases	Stretch wrapping Liquid proof coatings for card as used in products such as milk cartons Carrier and other plastic bags	When combined with card LDPE becomes a very versatile and cost-effective material Plastic bags perform well as an inexpensive method of producing a thin, protective layer for a wide range of goods
PP Polypropylene (Modelling material and commercial packaging material)	Very flexible – will withstand repeated folding Can be sterilised	Food containers Bags for dry food products such as pasta Bottle crates Slot-together boxes Yoghurt and margarine tubs Sweet and snack wrappers Video cases	Excellent chemical resistance means PP can be used where other plastics would be unsuitable Extremely tough and durable so will not break if dropped Flexibility and resistance to fatigue (wearing out) means that this material can be manufactured into boxes with 'integral' hinges which can be folded repeatedly without snapping or tearing
	CORRUGATED SHEET Available in corrugated sheet (plastic version of corrugated card sometimes referred to as Corriflute)	CORRUGATED SHEET Signage such as 'for sale' signs Architectural models Storage containers such as A3 folders	CORRUGATED SHEET Easily joined using specially designed components or hot melt glue
PS Polystyrene (Modelling material and commercial packaging material)	RIGID POLYSTYRENE Wide range of colours and transparent Stiff and hard Can be made impact resistant – High Impact Polystyrene (HIPS)	RIGID POLYSTYRENE Yoghurt pots CD cases Disposable cups and cutlery Bubble packs Prototype and architectural models	RIGID POLYSTYRENE Very suitable for vacuum forming
	EXPANDED POLYSTYRENE Excellent impact resistance Good heat insulator Very lightweight – very buoyant on water	EXPANDED POLYSTYRENE Take-away packaging Egg cartons Fruit, vegetable and meat trays Hot drink cups Protective packaging for electrical goods Expanded Polystyrene 'peanuts' are used to pack void spaces in boxes to prevent products moving in transit	EXPANDED POLYSTYRENE Does not add any significant weight to a packaged product As a good heat insulator, Expanded Polystyrene makes an excellent packaging material for hot food products Provides an excellent protective layer which absorbs impact preventing damage to valuable and fragile products
	FOAMBOARD Expanded Polystyrene sheet sandwiched between two layers of card, commonly 5 mm thick but also available in other sizes Rigid, easily cut and shaped, lightweight, suitable for drawing and painting, easily joined using hot melt glue or mapping pins	FOAMBOARD 3D models such as point-of-sale displays Architectural models Mounting 2D work for display	FOAMBOARD Can be cut more easily than card of similar thickness but still retains rigidity Quality card surface will accept a range of graphic media
	MODELLING FOAM (STYROFOAM) Available in fine textured blocks or sheets of various thickness Rigid, easily cut and shaped, lightweight, easily joined	MODELLING FOAM (STYROFOAM) Used to produce prototype models	MODELLING FOAM (STYROFOAM) When used as a modelling material Expanded Polystyrene can be shaped very easily and can be sanded to a smooth finish High quality, glossy finish possible by using filler, glass paper and by spray paint

Material	Significant properties	Uses	Advantages
Acetate (Modelling material)	Thin, transparent sheet Flexible	LCD screens for prototype models Windows for architectural models Windows in packaging Protective cover for 2D presentation drawings	Flexible Easily joined using hot melt glue Easily cut Transparent – available in clear or a range of tints Certain forms can be used in printers and photocopiers
Acrylic (Modelling material and commercial packaging material)	Wide range of bright colours Glossy finish Hard, brittle Rigid Heavy	High quality containers or closures for perfume products Signage Windows Point-of-sale displays	Available in a wide range of bright colours with a hard, glossy surface finish making it ideal for signage and products which require visual impact Little finishing required

Examination questions

 Q1 *Explain how and why you might use acetate and foamboard in an architectural model.*

4 marks

Acceptable answer

Foamboard: would be a suitable material to use for the **walls** of the model because it is **rigid**.

Acetate: because acetate is **clear**, it could be used to represent the **window glass**.

 Examiner's Tip

'Explain' requires you to justify the use of each material.

Q2 *Name **two** properties of Corrugated Polypropylene (Corriflute) which make it a suitable choice of material for making a slot-together A3 folder.*

2 marks

Acceptable answer

1 Durable.
2 Rigid.

WOOD

You need to know about:

☐ the common properties of wood which make it suitable for use as a modelling material

☐ the properties, working characteristics and applications of pine and MDF.

Wood can be classified into two groups:

• natural timbers – produced directly from trees, retaining natural grain and structure
• manufactured board – natural timbers processed to produce large uniform sheets.

KEY POINTS

COMMON PROPERTIES AND WORKING CHARACTERISTICS OF WOOD

Wood is used primarily as a modelling material because it is:

• versatile
• rigid
• low cost
• strong

• tough and durable
• recyclable
• suitable for many surface finishes, and
• it can be cut, planed, drilled and shaped relatively easily.

Wood can be shaped, formed and joined by:

• sawing
• chiselling
• planing

• drilling
• gluing

• jointing
• using nails and screws.

The properties, working characteristics and applications of pine and MDF

Material	Significant properties	Uses	Advantages
Pine	A naturally occurring timber Light brown or yellow colour Pronounced grain often with knots (grain will leave an impression on vacuum forming moulds)	General constructional work Vacuum forming moulds Architectural models Occasionally used for prestige packaging	Relatively inexpensive Easily shaped using a range of workshop tools and machinery Grain can be used to enhance visual appeal
MDF	A manufactured board Mid brown colour Available in a wide range of large uniform sheets Inexpensive Quite hard to shape (tends to blunt tools) Will swell if penetrated by moisture	General constructional work Vacuum forming moulds Architectural models Product modelling (Protection such as face masks and extraction are advisable when cutting which produces a very fine dust)	Uniform texture Can be glued together to form a solid block which can be shaped using a range of workshop tools and machinery A very smooth finish can be achieved which, once sealed and sanded lightly, provides an excellent surface for paint Impossible to obtain sheets this size from natural timbers

INDUSTRIAL APPLICATION

Jelutong is a natural timber which is often used for product modelling and making moulds. It has a very close grain, is very easy to shape, and is chosen by some designers in preference to pine and MDF.

Examination questions

Q1

Give **one** *reason why MDF would be chosen in preference to pine when making a vacuum forming mould.*

1 mark

Acceptable answer

Because the grain in a pine mould would show up on the finished product.

Q2

Describe **two** *stages in preparing the surface of an MDF model for spray painting. The model has already been cut into the correct shape.*

4 marks

Acceptable answer

1 I would first **sand the model** with coarse glass paper followed by smooth glass paper in order **to produce a smooth surface**.
2 Then I would **paint on two coats of sealant**, sanding lightly between coats to **stop the paint soaking into the wood**.

You need to know about:

☐ the common properties of metals which make them suitable for packaging

☐ the properties, working characteristics and applications of metals used in commercial packaging.

KEY POINTS

Steel and aluminium are commonly used for packaging products such as food and chemicals. They are also used to make closures such as bottle tops.

Metals are chosen for many reasons including:

- security
- strength
- durability
- can be heated to high temperatures
- can be cold formed and pressed into different shapes

- can be embossed
- labelling can be printed on directly or added as a different material
- visual impact – can be used to enhance appeal of a product.

Metals can be shaped, formed and joined by:

- cold forming
- cutting
- embossing
- welding
- gluing.

The properties, working characteristics and applications of metals used in commercial packaging

Material	Significant properties	Uses	Advantages
Aluminium	Impenetrable to air, light, moisture and germs Lightweight Strong Durable Usually lacquered to prevent unwanted reactions	Drinks cans (2- and 3-part cans) Pressurised aerosol containers Health and beauty products Closures such as bottle tops Aluminium foil closures Foil laminates combined with card to make cartons and other products	Good strength-to-weight ratio minimises material quantities required Aesthetic appeal – designers often retain the metallic finish of aluminium Manufacturing processes allow for the use of tamper-proof closures Can be recycled economically Can be combined as a foil laminate with other materials to enhance properties of packaging Does not rust
Steel	Impenetrable to light Very strong Durable Usually coated with tin to prevent unwanted reactions (rusting) Can be heated to very high temperatures to make food safe	Pressurised aerosol containers Sealed, processed foods (2- and 3-part cans) Closures such as bottle tops Resealable packaging such as biscuit and paint 'tins' Adhesive and chemical bottles or cans Decorative gift products	Strength and durability of tin-plated steel ensure that long lasting products stay stable for years Manufacturing processes allow for the use of tamper-evident closures

Examination questions

 Q1 *Explain **two** reasons why aluminium foil is used in PET blister packs to package pharmaceutical products such as headache pills.*

Acceptable answer

1 The aluminium foil is **broken easily** to release the pills **showing how many pills have been used/showing if the pack has been tampered with**.

2 Aluminium will **accept a variety of printing processes** allowing the manufacturer to **display product information** on the packaging.

Q2 *Give **one** reason why steel is coated with other materials such as tin when used in packaging.*

Acceptable answer

To prevent corrosion (rust).

GLASS

You need to know about:

□ the properties, working properties and applications of glass.

KEY POINTS

Chemicals can be added to colour glass to improve visual impact.

Glass is commonly used to package food and drinks products. When heated, glass can be formed by:

• pressing   • casting   • blow moulding.

The properties, applications and advantages of glass

Significant properties	Uses	Advantages
Transparent **Available in a range of colours** **Heavy** **Fragile** **Can be heated to high temperatures** **Impenetrable to germs, moisture and air**	Drinks bottles Food jars	Relatively inexpensive Excellent product visibility Hygienic Can be heated to high temperatures to kill germs Impenetrable to germs, moisture and air Will not react with or flavour the product Reusable and recyclable Printable Aesthetic appeal – consumers like the look and feel of glass compared with other materials such as plastic

Examination questions

 *Name **two** properties of glass which can be disadvantages when using it for packaging.*

2 marks

Acceptable answer
Glass is **fragile** and **heavy**.

 *Name **two** different properties of glass which allow it to be used for packaging food and drinks. Give **one** reason why each property makes glass a suitable material.*

4 marks

Acceptable answer
Property: It is **completely transparent**.
Reason: The product is **clearly visible**/can **enhance visual appeal**.
Property: It can **withstand heating to high temperatures**.
Reason: This **kills germs** in the product and jar simultaneously during production.

TOPICS

You need to know:

☐ that the choice and fitness for purpose of materials and components depend upon the relationship between working properties, intended manufacturing processes and end use

☐ how anthropometric data and the principles of ergonomics affect choices made by designers

☐ how to justify the choice of materials, components and designs used in commercial products.

KEY POINTS

Choice and fitness for purpose need to be considered by the designer when selecting materials and components and when developing designs.

JUSTIFYING THE CHOICE OF MATERIALS

The choice and fitness for purpose of materials, components and designs depend upon five key factors. The designer needs to **justify** his or her choice of materials and components by referring to:

- aesthetic properties
- functional properties
- meeting users' needs
- meeting the requirements of the specification
- suitability for manufacturing techniques
- cost.

ANTHROPOMETRIC DATA AND ERGONOMICS

Anthropometrics is the study of human dimensions (measurements taken from the human body). These measurements can be used by the designer to ensure that products and environments are suitable for real people.

Ergonomics is the study of the relationship between humans and the products, systems and environments they use. Ergonomically successful designs use anthropometric data to ensure that products are the right shape and size.

When designing products designers need to consider such areas as:

- shape and form
- ease of use
- size
- weight
- colour
- noise
- texture and feel
- materials
- maintenance
- safety.

When designing environments designers need to consider such areas as:

- movement
- light
- smell
- temperature
- space
- visibility
- facilities
- furniture and fittings
- maintenance
- safety.

Choice and fitness for purpose

28

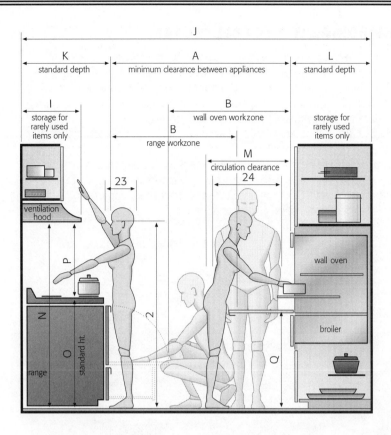

J

K — standard depth
A — minimum clearance between appliances
L — standard depth

I — storage for rarely used items only
L — storage for rarely used items only

B — wall oven workzone
B — range workzone
M — circulation clearance

23
24

ventilation hood

P

wall oven

broiler

range

standard ht.

N

O

2

Q

Anthropometric data used to produce an ergonomic environment

DESIGNING A PRODUCT: THE MICROSOFT INTELLIMOUSE

The Microsoft Intellimouse is particularly comfortable to use because a great deal of time was spent developing and testing alternative designs using different modelling methods. Eventually, the designers settled on an optimum form, size and weight for the mouse. The final design is very easy to use, incorporating a scroll wheel and well-positioned buttons. Optical sensors have replaced the traditional ball – mouse balls become dirty and impair performance. Optical sensors are more reliable and reduce the need for maintenance. Colour has been used to enhance the aesthetic qualities of the mouse – the internal components can be seen through a bright red, transparent base. Materials were selected such as the use of rubber-coated areas to enhance feel and grip. With minimal moving or detachable parts, the Intellimouse is very safe.

Prototype models exploring ergonomic shapes for a new mouse

Microsoft
Intellimouse
Explorer

Choice and fitness for purpose

29

DESIGNING AN ENVIRONMENT: THE CALL CENTRE

A well-designed ICT room, such as a call centre, will be large enough to allow staff to circulate freely. Large windows and strip lighting covered by diffusers will provide good lighting and ventilation. Heat will be controlled with the use of well-positioned radiators and air conditioning. Individual workstations will allow desk and storage space for every employee but the environment will be open plan to allow ease of communication between staff. Computer terminals will be positioned at the correct height and will be adjustable. Staff will be provided with adjustable chairs and furniture suitable for people of differing heights and weight. All furniture and equipment will be easy to remove for repair or replacement and the environment will be designed to enable cleaners to use their cleaning equipment easily. Toilet facilities and relaxation areas will be large enough to meet the needs of many staff. Furniture is selected without sharp corners and safety systems and equipment will be clearly identified and near at hand.

A call centre

KEY POINTS

Packaging is designed to:
- contain
- protect
- inform
- sell.

When justifying the choice of materials the designer has to refer to these.

PACKAGING AS A CONTAINER

Packaging is designed to hold a product. For example:
- Sealed milk cartons need to contain a liquid without leaking.
- The design of egg cartons allows the box to hold six eggs without touching.
- Aluminium cans are sealed to contain carbonated drinks.

PACKAGING TO PROTECT THE PRODUCT

Different products require different degrees of protection. This protection must last from the moment the product leaves the production line, through transport to the distributor and retailer, right up to the point where it is unpacked by the customer.

For example:

- Disposable surgical products require a sterile environment which provides protection from germs for a defined length of time.
- Injection moulded polystyrene foam is used to package large electronic products providing protection from impacts during transport and handling.
- Card, polythene and foil laminates are used in 'long-life' products to prevent light, air and gas permeating the packaging.

PACKAGING USED TO INFORM

A great deal of information is added to packaging. It is provided for the benefit of the consumer, retailer, distributor or manufacturer. It is a legal requirement for some information to be displayed.

For example:

- Food products must contain information such as weight and ingredients.
- Information contained in barcodes helps to speed up stock control and retailing systems.
- Plastic products display codes and symbols to help identification during recycling.

PACKAGING USED TO SELL THE PRODUCT

Manufacturers spend a lot of money on packaging in the hope that this will help to sell the product by making it more attractive to the consumer.

For example:

- Bottled drinks use transparent materials to display the product.
- Greens, blues and whites tend to dominate the packaging of cleaning products to suggest cleanliness, hygiene and fragrance.
- Battery packs are designed to hang on displays making them more visible to the customer.

EXAMPLE: JUSTIFYING THE CHOICE OF MATERIALS
The use of PET

PET is used for many fizzy drinks containers for a variety of reasons:

- Its aesthetic properties – PET can be manufactured with a glass-like transparency to enhance the visual impact of the product.
- Its functional properties – PET is a durable material which will withstand shocks, wear and tear.
- It meets users' needs. PET can be formed into bottles which, when combined with a plastic screw top, allow the customer to reseal the product. The bottle is an ergonomic shape which feels comfortable in the hand.

A bottle made of PET

- It meets the requirements of the specification. PET will meet the requirements of most specifications, for example it will not affect the flavour of the drink.
- Its suitability for manufacturing techniques – PET can be blow moulded. Pre-existing bottle designs and moulds can be used to reduce costs.
- PET is a cost-effective material. Due to its strength, relatively little material is required to produce an effective product.

Examination questions

Q1 *Explain **one** way in which anthropometric data would be used to help in the design of a mobile phone.*

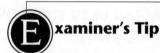

Acceptable answer
Finger measurements would be used to make sure that the **buttons were spaced for easy use**.

xaminer's Tip

One mark is awarded for correctly identifying an anthropometric measurement, the other mark is awarded for explaining how this data would be used.

Q2 *Packaging is designed to contain, protect, inform and sell. Explain **one** way in which egg cartons perform each of these functions.*

8 marks

Acceptable answer
Contain: Egg boxes **contain eggs separately** using **individual compartments and a self-locking lid**.

Protect: The **material used will absorb minor impacts** and allows some **stacking** of the product with careful handling.

Inform: **Card can be printed** and allows **information such as the barcode** to be included directly onto the box.

Sell: The material can be **coloured** to increase **visual impact**/the **carton design** allows **room for promotional graphics** to help sell the product.

xaminer's Tip

'Explain' requires you to justify each point in your answer. There are 8 marks so you can assume that you need to provide at least one justified point for each of the four functions.

You need to know:

☐ about cutting processes

☐ about the process of risk assessment in relation to the use of scalpels

☐ about general workshop safety issues.

KEY POINTS

- Through your project work you will have used a wide range of equipment. You should be able to describe the safe use of scissors, hot wire cutters, scalpels, safety rules and cutting mats.

- It is a statutory requirement for employers and other organisations such as schools to carry out risk assessments in order to eliminate or reduce the chances of accidents happening. You need to be able to carry out a risk assessment on the use of a scalpel with a safety rule and cutting mat. There are five steps:

  1 Identify the hazard.

  2 Identify people at risk.

  3 Evaluate the risk.

  4 Decide on control measures.

  5 Record assessment.

- In addition to the specific safety issues which should be observed when using materials, equipment and processes, you should be aware of general safety rules.

CUTTING

Tools and equipment	Uses	Safety
Scissors	Paper, thin card and thin plastic	Take care when carrying Keep fingers away from blades and cutting edges
Scalpel, safety rule and cutting mat	Paper, card and thin plastic and foam board more accurate than scissors	Ensure blade is sharp Cut away from body Always use safety rule Take care when carrying
Hot wire cutters	Cutting expanded/rigid foam plastic	Use in well-ventilated area Keep hands away from wire

EXAMPLE OF A RISK ASSESSMENT

Risk assessment for using scalpels

Hazard	People at risk	Risk	Control measures
Using a scalpel for cutting	Student	Cutting fingers or hand when cutting Cutting others when carrying scalpel	Ensure blade is sharp to reduce the need to apply excessive pressure Always cut away from body Always pay full attention when cutting Use **safety rule** (to protect fingers) and **cutting mat** Cover blade when not in use

Employers are responsible for the health and safety of their employees in the workplace.

GENERAL SAFETY RULES

- Make sure you have been trained in the use of the equipment that you intend to use.
- Wear appropriate protective clothing including eye protection.
- Use appropriate equipment for the task.
- Do not use electrical equipment near water.
- Turn off electrical equipment when finished.
- Be careful of trailing cables.
- Ensure others are aware of any safety issues.
- Ensure you know the emergency procedures.
- Ensure you are aware of the location of safety equipment including emergency stops and exits.
- Make sure you have enough workspace for the task.
- Use extraction equipment where available.
- Take care when carrying equipment.
- Take precautions when equipment is not in use.
- Report and refrain from using faulty equipment.

Examination questions

 Q1 *Carry out a risk assessment for using a hot-wire cutter by filling in the table below.*

 6 marks

Risk assessment for using a hot wire cutter

Hazard	People at risk	Risk	Control measures
Using a hot wire cutter to shape polystyrene foam	Operator Other students	• .... • .... •	• .... • .... • ....

Acceptable answer

Risks:

1 Fumes can be harmful.
2 Hot wire will cause burns if touched.
3 Electric shock if cable faulty.

Control measures:

1 Use in well-ventilated areas.
2 Keep fingers away from wire and switch off after use.
3 Check cable before use.

xaminer's Tip

These points do not form a complete list. Other valid risks and control measures would be awarded marks.

You need to know how:

☐ to describe the process of making basic prototype models and mock-ups.

KEY POINTS

Designers need to produce models in order to test their designs. Investing time and money at this stage will save money in the long run because it is much cheaper to correct mistakes and refine designs before production starts. Examples of the model making process are given below.

INDUSTRIAL APPLICATION

Modelling is also carried out on computers which can simulate tests

MAKING PRODUCTS, SUCH AS PACKAGING NETS, USING CARD

Remember that graphics should be added while the net is **flat**, before it is folded.

3D card modelling

Stages	Materials and equipment
1 Mark out nets	Drawing instruments, pencil
2 Add graphics and lettering	Coloured pens, pencils, transfer lettering
3 Score card	Scalpel, safety rule, cutting mat
4 Cut card and remove waste	Scalpel, safety rule, cutting mat, scissors
5 Add adhesive to tabs	Double-sided tape or glue stick
6 Assemble	

MAKING PRODUCTS, SUCH AS PROTOTYPE SOLID MODELS, USING POLYSTYRENE FOAM AND MDF

Remember that you need to seal materials to ensure a good finish.

3D solid modelling

Stages	Materials and equipment
1 Mark out side view	Pen
2 Cut	Hotwire cutter, scroll saw, coping saw
3 Mark out plan view	Pen
4 Cut	Hotwire cutter, scroll saw
5 Shape	Surforms, files, coarse glass paper
6 Sand smooth	Glass paper
7 Seal	Filler, emulsion paint
8 Add (aesthetic) components	Polystyrene lettering, self-adhesive paper labels
9 Spray	Aerosol spray (enamel paint)
10 Add details	Dry letter transfers, vinyl lettering

Professional modellers are used in many industries including the film industry

MAKING PRODUCTS, SUCH AS POINT-OF-SALE DISPLAYS, USING ACRYLIC

Remember that acrylic comes with a protective coating which should not be removed until necessary.

3D modelling using sheet plastics

Stages	Materials and equipment
1 Mark out net	Permanent felt tip or scriber, try square, steel rule
2 Cut and drill	Scroll saw, coping saw, band saw, pillar/bench drill
3 File edges	File
4 Sand edges	Wet and dry paper
5 Polish edges	Polishing machine
6 Bend to shape	Strip heater
7 Add graphics	Vinyl lettering, dry transfer letters

MAKING PRODUCTS, SUCH AS ARCHITECTURAL MODELS, USING FOAM BOARD

Remember that you should try to specify the correct form of adhesive.

3D modelling using foam board

Stages	Materials and equipment
1 Mark out foam board	Drawing instruments, pencil
2 Cut foam board	Scalpel, safety rule, cutting mat
3 Add components	Glue (type depends upon component)
4 Add graphics	Spray mount glue, dry transfer letters
5 Assemble	Mapping pins, hot glue

MAKING 2D PRODUCTS SUCH AS MENUS AND PRODUCT LABELS

2D laminated mock-ups

Stages	Materials and equipment
1 Scan original artwork	Scanner
2 Combine text and images	DTP software
3 Print	Inkjet or laser printer
4 Trim to size	Rotary cutter, guillotine or scalpel, safety rule and cutting mat
5 Laminate	Laminating machine or self-adhesive clear plastic film

Modelling

Examination questions

Q1 *Name **three** pieces of equipment which are needed to score card.*

3 marks

Acceptable answer
Scalpel, cutting mat, safety rule.

Q2 *Explain **one** reason why graphics should be added to 3D packaging nets before they are folded and assembled.*

2 marks

Acceptable answer
It is much **easier to work accurately** on a flat piece of card because **drawing instruments can be used/the surface remains solid**.

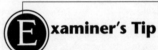

Examiner's Tip

One point with a linked reason is required here.

You need to know about:

☐ the safe use of permanent and temporary adhesives

☐ the range of non-industrial, 'functional' components which can be used to join modelling materials.

KEY POINTS

Most adhesives are designed to produce permanent joints which cannot be separated without damaging the materials. Many of these adhesives can prove harmful if used inappropriately, and you should be aware of the most important safety issues.

Some joints are designed to be temporary, allowing materials and components to be disassembled as and when required.

JOINING: ADHESIVES

Permanent and temporary adhesives

Adhesive	Description	Uses	Advantages	Safety
Glue stick	Solid stick of glue in 'lipstick' dispenser	Sheet materials Paper, thin card and thin plastic	Permanent Convenient dispenser system makes it easy to use and store	Most products completely non-toxic and safe
Spray mount	Aerosol container	Thin sheet materials Paper, card	Temporary, allows repositioning Does not crinkle paper Produces even coverage Quick dry Convenient aerosol	Flammable Pressurised container Use in well-ventilated area Avoid contact with skin and eyes
Hot melt glue	Available in sticks and used with hot glue gun	Paper and boards Plastic, metal, wood – most materials	Usually permanent Hardens quickly so suitable for rapid construction Does not form particularly strong joint so can be used for temporary joints Ease of application, versatile	Use stand Use mat Do not use near water Be careful of trailing cable Allow to cool before touching
PVA adhesive	'White' glue Liquid Available in a range of forms	Wood Paper and card (but moisture content will cause crinkling/warping)	Permanent When used properly (pressure needs to be applied) produces a very strong joint	Wash hands after use
Contact adhesive	Available in various forms. Commonly viscous, solvent-based liquid	Sheet materials Board, wood, metal, plastics	Permanent Allows dissimilar materials to be joined Allows flexibility in joints	Use in well-ventilated area Flammable Avoid contact with skin and eyes
Epoxy adhesive	Two-part adhesive Resin is mixed in equal parts with hardener	Most materials Particularly suitable for metal and plastic	Permanent Chemical reaction produces a very strong joint Allows dissimilar materials to be joined	Irritant Flammable Avoid contact with skin and eyes
Tensol cement	Strong smelling Thick, solvent-based liquid in metal can	Acrylic	Permanent When applied correctly produces a very strong joint	Use in well-ventilated area Irritant Flammable Avoid contact with skin and eyes

INDUSTRIAL APPLICATION

New technologies have led to the development of new adhesives such as environmentally friendly glues based on sugar.

FUNCTIONAL COMPONENTS

Components are used to join a variety of materials. All the examples shown in the table below form temporary joints which can be easily disassembled. Some of these components can be used in conjunction with adhesives to form permanent joints by holding materials in place while the adhesive sets.

Component	Description	Uses	Advantages
Paper fasteners	Brass-coloured steel split fasteners	Creating pivots for card mechanisms or ergonome models	Join is temporary When used correctly paper fasteners allow card to pivot freely
Paper clips	Available in different sizes and finishes	Used to join paper or card	Join is temporary
Drawing pins	Available in different sizes and finishes	Attaching presentation work to display boards	Join is temporary
Mapping pins	Plastic headed steel pins, available in different colours	Attaching presentation work to display boards Indicating positions of important information, i.e. on maps or diagrams Securing joints in foam board while waiting for glue to set	Join is temporary Easy to handle because of plastic head
Comb binder	Spiralling plastic or steel spine available in a range of sizes and colours	Binds documents into presentation booklets A special comb-binding machine is used to punch a series of holes along the edge of the document and to insert the comb binder forming a spine	Join is temporary An inexpensive and effective binding process for small batches

Modelling: joining materials

Examination questions

Q1 *Describe **two** safety precautions which should be taken when using epoxy resin.*

4 marks

Acceptable answer

1 Epoxy resin is an **irritant** so it is important to avoid contact with the skin by **wearing disposable gloves**.
2 Epoxy resin is **flammable** so it is important to **avoid using this adhesive near a naked flame**.

Examiner's Tip

Describe two stages and two safety issues. Ensure that each of your points is expanded. For example: 'Epoxy resin is an irritant ... avoid contact with skin.'

Q2 *Name **one** suitable method for binding a small batch of 200-page booklets.*

1 mark

Acceptable answer

Comb binders.

You need to know about:

☐ the purpose of applying surface finishes

☐ methods of surface preparation applied to common modelling materials

☐ the range of methods and materials available to the designer, used to apply surface finishes to models, and the safe and appropriate use of these finishing processes.

☐ the range of non-industrial, 'aesthetic' components which can be used to enhance the visual impact of prototype models.

KEY POINTS

There is a wide range of finishes available for the product designer. You need to be able to recommend suitable and appropriate finishes for modelling materials.

THE PURPOSE OF APPLYING SURFACE FINISHES

Finishes are applied to models in order to enhance their:

• aesthetic properties   • functional properties.

For example, varnish is used to enhance the look of wood, giving it a glossy finish. It also provides a strong, waterproof and protective layer which can be wiped clean.

PREPARATION OF MODELLING MATERIALS

For paper and boards, no preparation is required, although some thinner papers can be 'stretched' (taped to a board while wet) before applying paint, to prevent 'crinkling'.

For wood:

• Flat surfaces should be planed.
• Major blemishes can be filled and sanded with wood filler.
• Minor blemishes such as scratches should be sanded (in direction of grain if using natural timber), using progressively finer grades of glass paper until smooth.
• Primer or sealant should be applied and sanded lightly, between coats, when dry.

For plastic:

• Deep scratches and saw cuts on edges should be filed.
• A smooth finish is achieved by using progressively finer grades of wet and dry paper with a little water.
• A polishing machine may be used to achieve a shiny finish. (Most of the time plastics, such as acrylic, are selected for their naturally shiny finish which can be protected by leaving the protective coverings in place. If paint is to be applied, the surface should be 'keyed' by rubbing with fine wet and dry paper.)

Applying finishes to models

Finishing method	Description	Uses	Advantages	Safety
Sealant, primer and undercoat	Various liquid products Used to provide suitable surface for application of other finishing products	Woods, metals and plastics	Produces optimum surface for final paint finish	
Gloss and emulsion paints	Plastic and oil-based paints Requires a smooth, clean, surface free from dust and grease Primer usually needs to be applied Plane or sand to smooth finish and apply in thin coats, sanding lightly between applications	Woods	Cheap and easy to apply	
Enamel spray paint	Available in aerosol cans Requires a smooth, clean, surface free from dust and grease Woods need to be primed or sealed Metals and plastics should be primed	Woods, metals, plastics	High quality finish giving the appearance of plastic	Use in well-ventilated area Use extraction equipment if available Avoid contact with eyes and skin Wash hands after use Some artist quality pigments can be toxic
Varnish	Plastic-based clear and tinted liquids Requires a smooth, clean, surface free from dust and grease Plane or sand to smooth finish and apply in thin coats, sanding lightly between applications	Woods	Attractive, clear and glossy finish Strong protective coating	
Wood stain	Water- or spirit-based coloured liquid Requires a smooth, clean, surface free from dust and grease Plane or sand to smooth finish and apply with a rag or brush	Woods	Available in a range of colours Retains pattern of the wood grain	
Airbrush inks	Tinted liquids available in a wide range of colours Used with masking film	Papers and boards	Attractive finish for larger areas Colours and tones can be merged gradually	
Fixative	Clear aerosol spray	Papers and boards	Binds powdery material such as chalk so that it does not rub off	
Acrylic paints	Thick plastic-based opaque paints available in a wide range of colours Applied with brushes	Most materials	Dries to a durable, colourfast and waterproof finish	

Finishing method	Description	Uses	Advantages	Safety
Polishing machine	Saw cuts should be removed with a file and finished with wet and dry paper A polishing machine will finish acrylic to a bright shine	Plastics	Attractive, glossy finish	Wear goggles Do not touch moving parts Use correct part of wheel
Laminating	Paper and thin cards can be sealed in plastic sleeves using a laminating machine	Papers and boards	Protective and attractive finish	General precautions for using electrically powered equipment

Aesthetic components

Component	Description	Uses	Advantages
Modellers' raised plastic letters	Small white polystyrene letters Available in many styles and sizes	Can be glued to prototype models	When sprayed the lettering gives the appearance of having been part of the moulding process during manufacture
Self-adhesive paper labels	Widely available sheets of self-adhesive labels ('stickers') Available in many different shapes and sizes	Can be stuck onto prototype models	When sprayed the 'stickers' give the appearance of low-relief texture formed as part of the moulding process When added after spraying stickers can be used to simulate printed detail
Dry transfer letters	Rub down lettering, numbers or shapes Available in a range of styles, colours and shapes	Can be added wherever precise lettering is required such as prototype or architectural models	Easy to apply simulating printed detail

Examination questions

 Give **two** precautions you should take when using solvent based finishes such as varnishes.

Acceptable answer

1 Use in well-ventilated area.
2 Avoid contact with eyes and skin.

Examiner's Tip

General answers such as 'wear goggles' will not score marks.

Q2

*Describe **three** ways in which designers can enhance the aesthetic appearance of their models by applying surface detail and textures.*

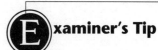
6 marks

Acceptable answer

1 Modellers' **raised plastic letters** can be glued carefully onto the model prior to painting to **give the impression of being part of the moulded casing**.

2 **Self-adhesive paper labels** can be stuck onto the model at the same time to give the **impression of moulded texture**.

3 After the model has been painted, **dry transfer letters and shapes** can be applied by rubbing to give the **impression of printed detail**.

Examiner's Tip

Make sure that you describe **how** each component enhances the aesthetic appearance of models.

You need to know:

☐ about the factors which influence the designer when selecting a manufacturing process

☐ how designers adapt existing designs and make use of pre-manufactured components

☐ about testing accuracy of prototypes against specifications and fitness for purpose

☐ how designers need to adapt designs when manufacturing in volume and plan to ensure quality

☐ how designers make efficient use of materials using lay planning.

KEY POINTS

It requires a great deal of investment to set up a manufacturing process. Machines have to be adjusted for new products and new equipment such as moulds may have to be commissioned. Any changes, which are needed after this, will be very expensive. As a result, designers are careful to get their designs right.

CHOOSING A MANUFACTURING PROCESS

A variety of factors influence the choice of manufacturing processes:

• **Materials used** – e.g. some papers and card are not available in rolls, so cannot be used in web-fed processes.

• **Quantities of product required** – the designer needs to choose between one-off, batch and volume manufacturing processes, e.g. it would not be sensible to use injection moulding to produce a one-off product.

• **Quality of finish required** – e.g. gravure will be selected in preference to other processes when very high quality prints are required.

• **Costs of the process** – e.g. it takes a great deal of money to set up the blow moulding process but once set up it is inexpensive to run.

• **Speed of production** – e.g. it takes much more time to produce hand-painted signs than to produce them using a CNC vinyl cutter.

• **Environmental and moral considerations** – e.g. companies may decide to choose processes which cause less harm to the environment, such as those which can make use of recycled materials.

EXAMPLE: CHOOSING THE MANUFACTURING PROCESS FOR A PLASTIC BUBBLE PACK

When developing a new plastic bubble pack the designer will be aware that the product will need to be produced in high volumes requiring a fast, automated process. PET is selected because of its transparency. Vacuum forming is chosen as the manufacturing process because it can produce large quantities of products quickly and is suitable for use with sheet PET. This means that the designer will have to incorporate a 'draft' angle into the design, so that the mould can be removed easily.

ADAPTING EXISTING DESIGNS

Many products are very similar and differ only in their graphic identity. For example, drinks companies use the same manufacturers who mass produce identical aluminium cans. Only the printed design on the cans will be different. Standard net designs are available which can be adapted by changing the dimensions to suit the new product. Standard pre-manufactured components are used such as closures for cartons.

Advantages include:

- tried and tested designs

- reduced design and manufacturing costs.

- mass and continuous production can be used where identical products are produced in large quantities, along production lines which can work non-stop, e.g. pharmaceuticals packaging.

DESIGNING FOR VOLUME MANUFACTURE

The designer needs to choose a suitable manufacturing process. This depends upon the quantity of products required and the materials which will be used. The designer will have to adapt any designs to suit the chosen manufacturing process. For example, when developing graphics, which are to be printed directly onto aluminium cans, the designer has to consider costs. It is very expensive to print more than a few colours so the designs need to be simplified.

The designer needs to take account of costs by ensuring that his or her designs will make full use of the materials and processes selected.

It is also important to plan quality control procedures. This often takes the form of a flow chart.

TESTING METHODS

Examples of testing methods include the following:

- Computer modelling – 'virtual' prototypes are tested using a range of specialist software (e.g. virtual crash tests). Using CNC equipment (such as modern CNC milling machines or stereo lithography), it is also possible to create solid, full-sized models directly from computer-generated designs.
- Virtual reality – environments such as buildings can be viewed from all angles.
- Test marketing – consumers are asked to evaluate a prototype.
- Wind tunnels – can test aerodynamic shapes.
- Testing to destruction – prototypes are tested for properties such as strength, using a range of specialist equipment.
- Specially produced templates or gauges – to test critical dimensions and tolerances.

LAY PLANNING OF PACKAGING PRODUCTS

The packaging material will be introduced into the manufacturing process in sheet form or from a large roll. The designer can adapt non-critical dimensions to ensure as much of the material is used as possible to minimise waste.

When packaging products have been printed and the required finishes have been applied, the designs need to be creased, scored and cut to shape. The designer will normally build tolerances into the packaging so that exact registration during die cutting is not essential, minimising quality control failures.

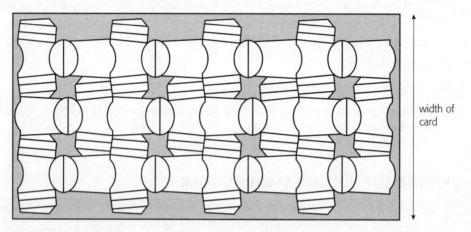

width of card

Efficient lay planning minimises waste for fast food chip cartons

Examination questions

Q1 *Describe **one** way in which designers can reduce the cost of producing card boxes through efficient lay planning.*

2 marks

Acceptable answer

They can **design nets which fit closely together (tessellate well)** and **which use as much of the card sheet or roll as possible** to minimise waste and reduce costs.

Q2 *Give **two** ways in which designers benefit from the availability of pre-manufactured packaging components.*

2 marks

Acceptable answer

1 They are proven designs.
2 They reduce design and manufacturing costs.

You need to know about:

☐ the principles of commercial printing and finishing processes

☐ a range of commercial printing processes and their application

☐ a range of commercial enhancing and finishing processes which can be applied to paper and board

☐ closure methods used in packaging.

KEY POINTS

You need to understand the general principles of commercial printing and finishing processes:

- process printing and colour separation
- spot colour
- registration
- sheet and web-fed processes.

You need to understand individual printing and finishing processes:

- letterpress
- lithography
- gravure
- screen printing
- photocopying
- die cutting and folding
- varnishing
- laminating
- embossing

You should also be aware of examples of commercial packaging.

COMMERCIAL PRINTING AND FINISHING PROCESSES

Commercial printing and finishing processes are applied in order to enhance or add to:

- the aesthetic properties of materials
- the functional properties of materials.

For example, card packaging can be varnished in order to give a high quality, glossy appearance or laminated to improve its durability.

It is important to select the most appropriate printing process. Designers need to consider:

- the material to be printed
- the scale of the print run required
- the quality of reproduction required
- the range of colours required
- the setting up and running costs of each process
- the speed of each process.

More colours generally mean more cost. By limiting the number of different colours in a design, costs can be kept to a minimum.

In order to contain and protect the product, packaging needs to be sealed. Depending upon the requirements of the product the designer will select temporary, permanent and/or resealable closures. Food products, for example, need to be sealed to prevent contamination but often include resealable features, such as screw tops, which continue to provide a more limited form of protection.

PROCESS PRINTING AND COLOUR SEPARATION

Processes such as lithography use the 'four-colour process' where the image to be printed has to be divided photographically, or using a computer, into its four constituent colours. This is called 'colour separation'. The colours are:

- cyan (blue)
- magenta (red)
- yellow
- black.

Four separate plates are produced which overlay each colour on paper, combining them to form the original image with the full range of colours and shades.

SPOT COLOUR

Where precise colours need to be produced, the four-colour process can be expanded to include 'spot colours' which are mixed and printed separately.

REGISTRATION

Where printing processes require the printer to print colours separately it is important to align them on the paper exactly. The process of aligning the plates is called 'registration'.

Registration and colour quality can be checked automatically using optical sensors.

SHEET AND WEB-FED PROCESSES

There are two means of introducing the material to be printed:

- Sheet-fed processes print onto individual sheets.
- Web-fed processes print onto a continuous roll which is cut up later.

Web-fed processes are quicker and more economical but more complicated to set up. As a result, these processes are ideal for the long print runs required for products such as newspapers.

Printing processes

Process	Description	Uses	Advantages
Letterpress	Relief printing process using a flexible metal or plastic plate High cost Slow process so usually employed for short runs Limited to one or two colours	Text in books Letterheads and business cards	Dense, opaque inks can be used to produce very high quality prints so ideal for products like business cards which need visual impact but do not require a range of colour
Flexography	A form of letterpress. Relief printing process using a flexible rubber plate wrapped around a cylinder Relatively inexpensive to set up High speed Can use same presses as letterpress process	Less expensive magazines Paperbacks Newspapers Packaging including plastics, foil laminates, paper and boards	Versatile so can be used on a wide range of materials unsuitable for other processes such as foil/film laminates Cheap setting up costs and high-speed print runs make flexography ideal for newspapers which change daily

Process	Description	Uses	Advantages
Lithography	Based upon the principle that water and oil do not mix. Rollers apply image to paper. Good quality reproduction, especially photographs, using the four-colour process although colour can vary due to water and dyes used Inexpensive High speed Not suitable for all types of paper due to water used	Business cards and stationery Brochures Posters Magazines Newspapers Packaging including plastics, paper and boards	Wide range of machines available, small and large, so suitable for short and long runs Good quality photographic reproduction make lithography a widely used process
Gravure	Image is etched onto copper plate using a photographic process Consistent, high quality colour reproduction Very expensive to produce printing plates so more suitable for long runs High speed Can be used on paper unsuitable for lithography	High quality books and magazines Postage stamps High quality packaging including plastics, paper and boards	Excellent quality of reproduction is the main reason for selecting this process. Because of this gravure is often used for expensive art books and prints
Screen printing	Colours are forced through screens which contain stencils to produce areas of colour Inexpensive to set up so suitable for short runs Fast commercial machines available Suitable for most materials	T shirts Posters Card, plastic and metal signage Point-of-sale displays	Thick opaque inks are good for simple designs with blocks of colour rather than fine detail Inexpensive to set up so suitable for short runs of custom-made products such as one-off event signage
Photocopying	A dry printing process which relies on particles of toner being attracted to charged areas of the paper which is then heated to fix the image Inexpensive for short black and white runs. Colour copying is expensive No setting up time required Suitable for copier paper and heat resistant acetate	Reproduction of images, short documents Enlarging or reducing images and documents	As there is no need to spend time or money on setting up the process, the photocopier is an ideal means of producing single sheets and short documents

Industrial processes: printing and finishing

Examiner's Tip

You will not be asked directly about flexography but you may choose to refer to it in some of your answers

FINISHING PROCESSES
Print finishes

Material	Description	Uses	Advantages
Die cutting and folding	Machine cutting, creasing, scoring and folding of card	Brochures Packaging nets Unusually shaped papers and cards such as those needed for pop-up books	Once the die is made it can be used many times and is only suitable for products such as packaging boxes which are produced in longer runs
Ultraviolet (UV) varnishing	UV light is used to harden a liquid, plastic coating Can be used in selected areas (spot varnishing)	Glossy book covers Glossy packaging Glossy highlights	High gloss finish enhances visual impact Protects against scuffing, so keeps appearance for longer Can be applied at the same time as printing
Spirit varnishing and aqueous varnishing	Both finishes use a liquid during or after printing	Used as UV varnishing where high gloss finish is not required	Good, low-cost general purpose protective and enhancing finish Protects against scuffing Can be applied at the same time as printing
Laminating	Paper layer: • provides an excellent printing surface Aluminium foil layer: • enhances visual appeal • excellent air, light and moisture barrier for 'long-life' products Polythene or PET layer: • offers protection to the printed surface • acts as a good air and moisture barrier • adds durability and strength • provides an attractive glossy finish, enhancing visual appeal • allows product to be hygienically heat sealed	Many forms of packaging combine two or more material laminates, e.g. orange juice cartons, vacuum packed coffee packs, chocolate bar wrappers, chocolate boxes	By combining materials, the designer can unite the best characteristics of all three materials into a single package Hot foil blocking allows the designer to enhance visual impact by adding metallic finishes to selected parts of the design
Embossing	Raises part of the design above the surface of the flat material using an embossing die	A variety of packaging and publications	Enhances visual impact by emphasising areas of the design against the flat material Often combined with other processes such as hot foil blocking or spot varnishing

CUTTING, FOLDING, CREASING AND SCORING

- Straight line cuts are made using large industrial guillotines, which can process large quantities of paper or card.
- Folding – bending the material.
- Creasing – compressing the material along a line without breaking the surface.
- Scoring – cutting the surface of the material along a line.
- Both creasing and scoring improve the quality of the fold but scoring will weaken the material where it has been cut.

EXAMPLES OF CLOSURE METHODS USED IN COMMERCIALLY PRODUCED PACKAGING

Closure methods include:

- gluing – a permanent joint
- tacking – a glued joint which can be separated easily
- welding – a permanent joint used to seal plastic and laminated products
- slot-together closures – a reusable method
- use of standard components such as bottle tops, lids and spouts – often designed to be reusable
- tamper-evident closures – a wide range of methods, used in food and pharmaceuticals packaging, which shows if the product has been opened.

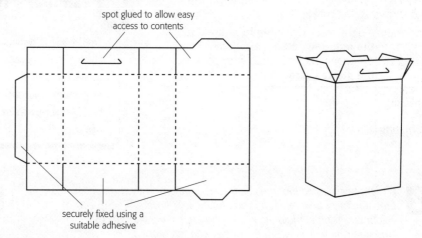

spot glued to allow easy access to contents

securely fixed using a suitable adhesive

Tacked permanent joins

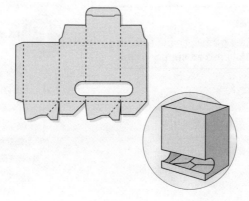

Slot-together closures

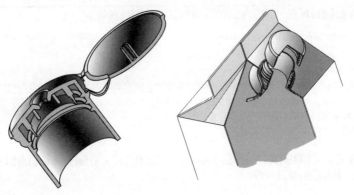

Standard closures

Examination questions

Q1 *Name the commercial process used to cut out playing cards and describe how it works.*

3 marks

Acceptable answer

Cutting process: Die cutting

Description: A die is made with a **blade, shaped to the required outline**. It is placed in the die-cutting machine which **stamps out the printed cards** to the required shape.

xaminer's Tip

One mark is awarded for naming the process correctly, the other two marks are awarded for a brief description of the process.

Q2 *A client has insisted that the colour of a company logo in a printed brochure must be exactly matched to the specification. The quality of colour is difficult to maintain in the lithographic printing process. Describe **one** way in which the printer can get around this problem.*

2 marks

Acceptable answer

By **using spot colour**, the printer can print the logo separately from a **specially mixed supply of ink**.

xaminer's Tip

One mark is awarded for correctly identifying the process, the other mark is awarded for a brief description of the process.

You need to know about:

☐ the principles and stages of commercial plastic forming processes

☐ plastic forming processes used in school.

KEY POINTS

Thermoplastics can be shaped and formed using:

• line bending   • injection moulding   • blow moulding   • vacuum forming.

Some of these processes can be carried out in schools.

LINE BENDING

This process uses a strip heater to bend thermoplastic sheet materials such as acrylic. Products include point-of-sale displays and stands. This process is also commonly available in schools. The equipment uses either a heated wire, or an electric element to soften the plastic.

Process:

1 Wait until equipment reaches optimum temperature.

2 Place fold line on plastic into position and turn to prevent burning.

3 Wait until the fold softens.

4 Bend the plastic.

5 Wait until plastic has cooled.

6 Repeat process for other folds.

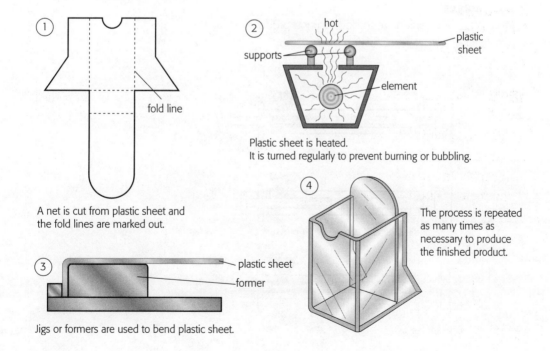

① fold line

A net is cut from plastic sheet and the fold lines are marked out.

② hot — plastic sheet — supports — element

Plastic sheet is heated.
It is turned regularly to prevent burning or bubbling.

③ plastic sheet — former

Jigs or formers are used to bend plastic sheet.

④ The process is repeated as many times as necessary to produce the finished product.

Advantages:
- Low cost.
- Suitable for small batch and one-off production.

Disadvantages:
- Even with use of jigs not as accurate as other processes.
- Not suitable for high volume production.

INJECTION MOULDING

Liquid plastic is forced into a mould which is cooled to produce a wide range of products such as casings for electronic products and closures for packaging.

Process:
1 Granules are poured into the hopper.
2 The granules are heated.
3 The screw pushes the softened granules forward.
4 The plasticised (melted) material is forced into the mould.
5 The mould is cooled (water flows through mould).
6 The ram is withdrawn, the mould opens.
7 The hardened product is ejected from the mould with ejector pins.
8 The mould closes and the process is repeated.

Advantages:
- Intricate detail and textures can be produced.
- Moulds produce accurate products.
- Highly automated process.
- Products require very little finishing.
- Suitable for high volume production.
- Low unit costs for long production runs.

Disadvantages:
- Moulds are very expensive to develop and produce.
- Not suitable for small production runs.

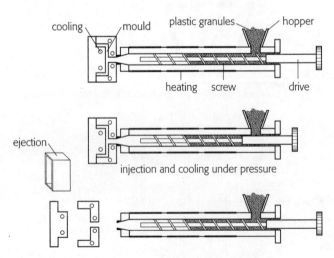

Injection moulding process

BLOW MOULDING

Air is blown into a sealed, pre-formed tube (parison) forcing the plastic into the sides of a split mould. The process is used to produce hollow containers such as plastic bottles.

Process:

1 An extruded parison is inserted into the split mould.

2 The split mould closes, sealing the parison at one end.

3 Hot compressed air forces the plastic into shape of mould.

4 The mould is cooled and the plastic hardens.

5 The mould opens and the product is ejected.

6 The process is repeated.

Advantages:

• Intricate shapes can be formed such as screw threads on bottles.

• Moulds produce accurate products.

• Highly automated process.

• Products require very little finishing.

• Suitable for high volume production.

• Low unit costs for large production runs.

Disadvantages:

• Moulds are very expensive to develop and produce.

• Not suitable for short production runs.

• Large amounts of waste created.

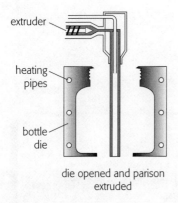

die opened and parison extruded

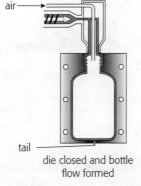

die closed and bottle flow formed

die opened after cooling and bottle formed

Blow moulding process

VACUUM FORMING

Plastic sheets are 'sucked' over a mould. The process is used to produce trays and containers such as chocolate-box trays, yoghurt pots and blister packs. This process is also available in schools and is commonly used to form HDPS sheets.

Process:

1 A mould is placed on the platen which is lowered.
2 A plastic sheet is clamped into place above the mould.
3 The heater is pulled over the plastic sheet.
4 When the plastic sheet has softened the platen is raised.
5 A pump expels the air which creates a vacuum causing the plastic to be forced over the mould.
6 The platen is lowered and the mould removed.
7 Waste material is trimmed.

Advantages:

• Ideal for batch production.
• Can be automated.
• Moulds can be modified.

Disadvantages:

• Difficult to achieve uniform thickness of material as it is stretched over mould. (Blowing air into the cavity to stretch the plastic before creating a vacuum can reduce problems.)
• Webbing will occur with poorly designed moulds.
• A draft angle needs to be incorporated into the design so the mould can be removed.
• Usually requires trimming or cutting to size.

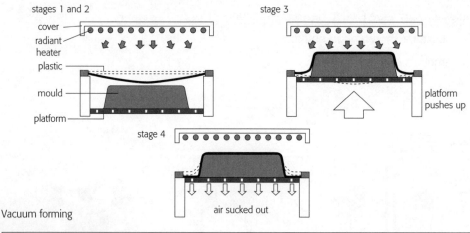

Vacuum forming

Examiner's Tip

You will not be required to draw the diagrams shown above from memory, but you should be able to describe the stages involved in each process.

Examination questions

Q1 *State **one** reason for the inclusion of a draft angle into the design of vacuum forming moulds.*

1 mark

Acceptable answer
So the mould can be removed from the finished product.

Q2 *Give **four** advantages of using injection moulding to produce products in volume.*

4 marks

Acceptable answer
1 It is a highly automated process.
2 Intricate detail and textures can be produced.
3 Moulds produce accurate products.
4 Products require very little finishing.

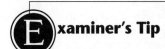

Examiner's Tip

'Give' does not require you to expand on your answers.

QUALITY

You need to know:

☐ how to recognise quality in existing products

☐ about the role tolerances and critical dimensions play in quality control

☐ how products are tested for quality

☐ about the role quality assurance plays in commercial organisations

☐ how quality control is used during manufacturing.

TOPICS

KEY POINTS

It is easy to recognise a quality product but more difficult to justify your opinion.

In order to analyse products effectively, it is necessary to judge quality against a range of criteria.

Tolerances and critical dimensions are specified by the designer to ensure quality. As part of quality assurance, quality control procedures are established to test products at regular intervals during the manufacturing process.

Product analysis involves applying the knowledge you have acquired in this subject and from other sources. The product and its components should be analysed, using the criteria below.

Designers analyse competing products thoroughly before developing new ones.

CRITERIA USED TO JUDGE THE QUALITY OF A PRODUCT

- **How it looks (aesthetics)**. How is the product made to look visually appealing?
- **How it performs (function)**. How well does the product work and what features make it work?
- **The needs and values of users and the market**. Does it appeal to the customer and will it perform as the customer expects?
- **Moral considerations**. Does the product harm or offend anyone associated with its manufacturing, sale, use or disposal?
- **Cultural considerations.** Does the product offend any sections of the population?
- **Environmental considerations**. Does the product help or harm the environment?
- **Materials used**. Have appropriate materials been used?
- **Processes used**. Have appropriate processes been used?
- **Safety**. Is the product safe for everyone who may come into contact with it?
- **Value for money**. Is the product the most cost-effective way of performing the task?

Quality

60

TOLERANCES, CRITICAL DIMENSIONS, SIZE AND FIT

Tolerances can be set for any property including:

- size
- weight
- colour
- strength.

Tolerance limits are expressed as a ± figure. For example, if the tolerance limit is set at ±0.02 for the thickness of acrylic sheet, all sheets between 4.98 and 5.02 would be accepted and those outside this tolerance would have to be scrapped.

Tolerance is the margin of error or degree of imperfection allowed in a product or component. Tolerances can be checked manually through visual inspections or by using sophisticated probes and sensors, and the data gathered analysed.

In most products some dimensions are more important than others. Dimensions which have to be accurate are known as critical dimensions. These will be checked regularly during the manufacturing process using measuring devices. This is especially important when pre-manufactured components need to be assembled into the product. If quality control fails, then these components will not fit together.

TESTING FOR QUALITY

Products, components and materials are tested at various stages during development, and includes:

- non-destructive testing
- destructive testing.

Aesthetic properties can be tested by conducting consumer surveys.

Non-destructive testing

This relies on techniques which do not harm or damage the product/component/material. For example, when testing critical dimensions, manual or automated equipment is used to measure selected dimensions. Components can be x-rayed to check for flaws using ultrasound or x-ray equipment, or scales can be used to check product weight.

Testing to destruction

Samples of the product are tested until they fail. For example, a sampled drinks bottle is pumped up with liquid to a high pressure to find out when it bursts in order to make sure that it is safe to use with fizzy drinks. Adding weights until the product collapses checks the stacking strength of cardboard boxes.

QUALITY ASSURANCE

Quality assurance is an overall approach adopted by a company to ensure that high quality standards are maintained throughout the organisation and suppliers. Every activity within a company – standards, procedures, documentation and communication systems – are established and monitored. This usually involves developing a quality manual which defines the best way of doing things and which can be followed by all staff.

QUALITY CONTROL

As part of quality assurance, quality control ensures high standards during production and aims to create a system with zero faults. It is achieved by setting up a system of inspection, checks and tests which will be carried out at all stages during manufacturing. It is important to plan these before production starts.

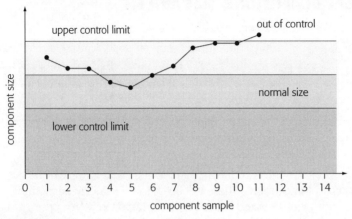

A quality control chart

It is often impossible to inspect every component so sampling is used where inspection takes place at planned intervals.

Results of inspections are gathered and analysed. It is often possible to use these data to predict when a particular machine needs adjustment or repair because accuracy in the components will drift gradually and the problem can be dealt with before components run out of tolerance.

This system of sampling and inspection can also identify batches of faulty materials and inaccurate machine operators.

Examination questions

Q1 *Explain the difference between quality assurance and quality control.*

4 marks

Acceptable answer

Quality assurance is concerned with **imposing international quality standards throughout an organisation**, from suppliers through to retailers. Quality control is concerned with **setting up systems and procedures to maintain quality in products** during manufacture.

Q2 *Describe **one** way in which sampling may be used to maintain quality in newspaper production.*

2 marks

Acceptable answer

Individual newspaper pages are **removed from the production line at regular intervals** so that **colour registration can be inspected**.

SINGLE-ITEM, BATCH AND VOLUME MANUFACTURE

You need to know about:

- ☐ the advantages, disadvantages and applications of single-item manufacture
- ☐ the advantages, disadvantages and applications of batch and volume manufacture.

KEY POINTS

ICT is used extensively in the manufacture of single-item products. Computer-assisted design (CAD) is used to create designs and computer numerical control (CNC) machines are used to translate these designs into components and products. Promotional products, such as leaflets and posters, look more professional when produced on desktop publishing packages.

Batch and volume manufacturing systems are chosen because they are very cost effective. Costs can be divided into:

- capital costs – the setting up costs, such as investment in buildings and machinery
- operational costs – the costs which are incurred once the system is operational such as wage bills and electricity bills
- unit costs – the total cost of producing one unit or product.

For example, the unit costs of mass-produced aluminium cans are low because they can be produced with minimal operational costs, using a low level of cheap unskilled labour and buying raw materials in bulk. The capital costs of setting up a large factory and production line, however, are very high and it takes many years before profits pay for the initial investment.

Scale of manufacture

Type	Description	Examples of uses	Advantages	Disadvantages
Single-item (one-off)	Single custom-made products requiring skilled, specialist craftspeople	Vinyl graphics for signs and transport livery Architectural models Movie props Shop and exhibition displays Packaging mock-ups 3D prototype models Graphic design mock-ups, e.g. posters, leaflets	Product can be made to very exacting specifications Low tooling costs Low capital (setting up) costs Design can be changed easily during production	Slow Labour intensive No economies of scale Skilled, specialist craftspeople often required Expensive materials and processes often used
Batch	Products produced in specified quantities. Production runs can be large or small. Companies can switch production to different products	Stationery Business cards Leaflets Brochures Posters Point-of-sale displays Promotional packaging	Flexible systems can be changed to produce different products easily Rapid response to changes in customer needs Easy to change size of batches Possible to adapt processes between batches Bulk buying of raw materials at lower prices	Advantages enjoyed by volume manufacture are sacrificed in order to achieve flexibility which leads to a slower, more expensive process and product

Type	Description	Examples of uses	Advantages	Disadvantages
Volume	Volume, mass or continuous production where identical products are produced continuously, in large quantities, along production lines which can work non-stop	Pharmaceutical packaging Aluminium cans Tin cans Standard plastic bottles and containers Standard card and paper products Plastic bags	Less labour and more automation lead to higher efficiency Work can be divided into simple, repetitive tasks suitable for cheap unskilled labour Rapid, non-stop production makes optimum use of capital investment Bulk buying of raw materials at lower prices All the above lead to lower unit costs and a cheaper product	Very expensive to purchase and set up specialised machinery Difficult to make big changes during production Social issues due to fewer jobs created and reliance on unskilled labour performing boring, repetitive tasks

Examination questions

 Q1 *Give **two** reasons why a batch-produced vinyl graphic would be less expensive to produce than a single item (one-off) vinyl graphic.*

2 marks

Acceptable answer

1 The cost of setting up the machines could be shared by the batch-produced products.

2 Raw materials could be bought in quantity at a lower price.

THE USE OF CAD/CAM AND ICT IN SINGLE-ITEM MANUFACTURE

You need to know:

- ☐ about the advantages of using CAD and CAM and CNC equipment

- ☐ about the range of software and resources available to the designer

- ☐ about the range of ICT hardware available to the designer

- ☐ how ICT is used in single-item manufacture

KEY POINTS

- The use of CAD, CAM and CNC equipment provides the designer and manufacturer with a number of advantages which speed up the development of products and help to ensure quality.

- A range of software applications, ICT resources and computer hardware help to make the work of the designer much easier.

- ICT is used extensively in the design and manufacture of one-off products such as vinyl graphics.

ADVANTAGES OF USING COMPUTERS TO DESIGN, I.E. COMPUTER-AIDED DESIGN (CAD)

- **Accuracy**. Even large and complicated designs can be drawn precisely, to very small tolerances, with all the information contained on a single drawing. This eliminates the need to produce a larger number of drawings.

- **Repeatability**. It is easy to reproduce identical features or components in drawings using copy and paste commands or by adapting pre-drawn components. This speeds up the design process.

- **Ease of modification**. Changes are very easy to make using editing tools and most software will adapt the rest of the design automatically to allow for these improvements. This speeds up the design process and encourages experimentation.

- **Ease of storage**. Designs can be stored and retrieved electronically on the network, on disk, on CD-ROM or by using a range of small electronic devices. This speeds up the design process, reduces storage space and can allow open access to files.

- **Ease of transport**. Multiple copies of a design can be created at the touch of a button and can be sent electronically across networks. It is even possible to have designers working simultaneously on the same file in different parts of the world.

- **Ease of testing**. Complicated tests can be carried out on-screen without the need to use expensive, destructive methods of testing.

- **Tools**. A wide range of specialist tools can perform complex operations quickly and automatically speeding up the design process.

- **Speed**. The software can carry out complex calculations automatically.

THE ADVANTAGES OF USING COMPUTERS TO MAKE, I.E. COMPUTER-AIDED/ASSISTED MANUFACTURE (CAM)

- **Speed**. Although CAM machines may seem slow sometimes, they work much faster than human beings.
- **Accuracy**. Even school-based CAM machinery will work to tolerances approaching $\pm \frac{1}{100}$th of a millimetre.
- **Repeatability**. It is easy to reproduce identical components.
- **Productivity**. More products can be produced because CAM machines can work continuously without the need for breaks.
- **Safety**. Since the operator is not in direct contact with the tools or materials, accidents happen rarely. CAM machines can work with dangerous materials.

CNC (computer numerical control) machines are controlled by computers (CAM), which generate numbers called G and M codes. These translate the design drawn on the computer screen into a language which will be understood by the CNC machine.

Examples of CNC machines include:

- milling machines
- lathes
- routers
- vinyl cutters
- laser cutters.

Industrial CNC machines work on the same principles as those in schools but on a much larger scale.

There is a wide range of software available. It is important for the designer and manufacturer to make appropriate choices.

Computer software

Software applications	Description	Examples of uses	Advantages
CAD drawing software, e.g. TechSoft 2D Design, PTC ProDesktop, AutoCAD, TurboCAD	Generally refers to 2D and 3D technical drawing applications which are used to produce accurate, dimensioned working drawings. Used by engineers, product designers and architects, etc. • A product is drawn on screen • The structure is tested on screen • A rendered 3D drawing is created to test aesthetics • G and M codes are created and sent to a CNC milling machine • A 3D prototype is produced which can be handled to test ergonomics	Engineering drawings Architectural plans Packaging nets 3D models Designs for CAM equipment	Speed Accuracy Repeatability Ease of modification Ease of storage Ease of transport Ease of testing Range of tools

Software applications	Description	Examples of uses	Advantages
DTP, e.g. Microsoft Publisher, Serif PagePlus, Adobe PageMaker, QuarkXPress	Used by designers to layout publications • Text is word processed • Photographs, images and graphics are created digitally or commissioned from an illustrator and scanned to create digital images • The overall layout style is created in a DTP program and all the elements are combined • A proof copy is printed and checked (proof-read) before being sent to a commercial printing company	Books Newspapers Magazines Leaflets Business cards Posters Printed packaging designs Web pages	Text and images can be manipulated within program Wide choice of typefaces and clipart Layout tools such as guides can be used Manual processes such as zoom, cut and paste can be reproduced electronically Pre-designed templates can be used and a house style template can be created to produce standardised documents Documents can be spell checked
Draw, paint and photo applications, e.g. Microsoft Paint, CorelDraw, Serif DrawPlus, Serif PhotoPlus, Adobe Photoshop, Macromedia Freehand, JASC Paint Shop Pro, Adobe Illustrator	Used to create and manipulate visual images. Designs can be created from scratch or conventional images can be scanned into the program and manipulated using a wide range of tools. Photographs can also be introduced directly using a digital camera • Initial drawings are sent to client for approval • Once approval is given, the drawing is scanned and imported into the application • The image is traced on-screen to create a digital outline • The image can now be manipulated and colour can be added • A hard copy is printed	Web graphics Logos Magazine illustration Advertising images Photograph retouching	Designs can be modified easily Wide choice of typefaces and clipart Manual processes such as zoom, cut and paste can be reproduced electronically Wide range of tools available for use to create interesting effects automatically The image can be built up in layers which can be modified individually Most applications now include features to help in the creation of web graphics

INDUSTRIAL APPLICATION

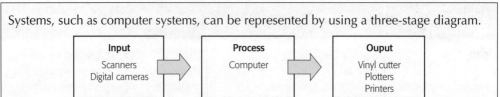

Systems, such as computer systems, can be represented by using a three-stage diagram.

Input	Process	Ouput
Scanners Digital cameras	Computer	Vinyl cutter Plotters Printers

Hardware

Input/output device	Description	Use	Advantages
Scanner (input device)	Allows the designer to input existing images and photographs, creating digital images which can be manipulated using different software applications • Image is placed in scanner • Image is scanned • Image appears on screen	Used to create digital images from existing images or artwork	Digitised images can be stored and transmitted more efficiently A wide range of software allows images to be manipulated on screen
Digital camera (input device)	Digital cameras do not use conventional film but store images in digital format which can be downloaded directly into the computer • Picture is taken • Picture is downloaded onto computer • Picture appears on screen	Used to create original digital images	Images can be incorporated into publications or web pages
Vinyl cutter (output device)	A CNC machine which can cut vinyl and card. Some can be used as plotters • Vinyl or card is clamped into plotter cutter • Drawing file is opened in CAD drawing program and sent to cutter • Design is scored and cut • Vinyl or card is removed • Waste is removed (weeding) • Application tape is used to apply design to product	Vinyl products such as: • transport livery • signage Card products such as: • pop-up card mechanisms • packaging nets	Accurate Quick Pressure of cut is adjustable to allow scoring Different coloured vinyls can be combined in one design
Plotter (output device)	Uses pens for cleaner, more accurate lines on larger drawings	Large technical drawings such as: • architectural plans • engineering drawings • final designs	Clean accurate line drawings Quick Automatically changes between different coloured pens Suitable for large drawings
Inkjet printer (output device)	Wide range of printers available which use ink to produce coloured prints Relatively slow Uses liquid inks which require drying time Expensive coated papers available for photo quality prints	Used widely at home and in schools	Low cost printer available High quality images at high resolutions Relatively low cost for average user Cheap method of obtaining colour prints
Laser printer (output device)	Available in black/white and colour. Faster models tend to be more expensive. Laser printers use toner powder which is fixed using pressure and heat	Used more in busier computer suites and offices	Very high quality print and very high resolutions Fast Will not smudge More cost effective over long term and more suitable for heavy usage

ICT IN SINGLE-ITEM MANUFACTURE: VINYL GRAPHICS

Sign making is a large industry which supports many businesses, large and small. These businesses produce custom-designed graphics for a wide range of purposes including signage and transport livery (vehicle graphics).

In this example, vinyl graphics are being produced for the delivery vans in a courier company:
- The designer meets with the client to discuss requirements and a specification is drawn up.
- The client is shown stock examples which are **stored on the computer**.
- To save time the client **emails** a **digital version** of the company logo.
- A design is developed on the computer using **CAD** drawing software and **emailed** to the client.
- The client approves the design and specifies colours and vinyl.
- The final design is sent to the large, industrial **CNC vinyl cutter** which cuts it out.
- The unwanted vinyl is removed from the design in a process called weeding.
- Application tape is applied to retain the correct spacing in the design.
- The design is now ready to be peeled off with the application tape and applied to the vehicle.

INDUSTRIAL APPLICATION

Rapid Prototyping allows ICT to control the whole design and manufacturing process from beginning to end

CLIPART

Clipart is the collection of pre-drawn images and symbols which can be inserted into documents. These are available in libraries which can organise thousands of copyright-free files into a manageable structure.

CD-ROMS

Compact disks (CD-ROMs) contain encyclopaedias, programs and libraries of specialist symbols, which can be used by the designer. ROM stands for 'Read Only Memory' which means the information on the disks cannot be changed.

THE INTERNET

The world wide web, also known as the Internet, is a rich resource for information. It consists of a huge collection of linked web pages written in a language called HTML. Wise use of search engines can give the designer instant access to a wide range of information or design resources.

The growth of the Internet has led to increased demand for web designers who use specialist software to create web pages.

Examination questions

Q1

*Name **two** resources which could be used to obtain images when using a computer.*

2 marks

Acceptable answer
1 CD-ROM
2 Internet websites.

Q2   *Describe **three** advantages of using computer-aided design.*

6 marks

Acceptable answers

Any three from the following:

Changes are very easy to make using the **editing tools**.
After editing, the **software will adapt the rest of the design automatically** to accommodate improvements, **speeding up the design process**.

Designs can be stored and retrieved electronically which **saves space** and **allows easier/quicker access to drawings**.

Multiple copies of a design **can be created at the touch of a button** allowing **repeated features to be duplicated easily**.

Designs can be sent instantly across **global networks**. This allows designers to **work simultaneously on the same file in different parts of the world**.

Examiner's Tip

One advantage and one effect must be provided for each of the three advantages.

You need to know how:

☐ ICT is used in the management of product and design data

☐ ICT is used in the management of electronic communications

☐ ICT is used in production control

☐ ICT is used to manage stock control

☐ ICT is used in quality control

☐ a product is batch produced

☐ a product is produced in volume.

KEY POINTS

ICT is used to help manage product and design data:
- 3D modelling software can be used to demonstrate and manipulate 'virtual' designs
- it is much easier to store and retrieve electronic data.

ICT helps people to communicate through the use of:
- email
- Internet
- video conferencing.

ICT is used to control production through:
- CIM (computer integrated manufacture)
- remote manufacturing.

ICT helps to manage stock through:
- automated stock control systems
- EPOS systems

ICT helps to manage quality control automatically:
- in the printing industry.

ICT is used extensively in the manufacture of:
- batch-produced business cards
- volume-produced newspapers and magazines.

MANAGING PRODUCT AND DESIGN DATA

Virtual Prototyping

Virtual prototyping is a technology which is used to model designs in three dimensions (3D) on screen. Products can be prototyped before a 3D model is commissioned. They are built up as a simple 'wire frame' model which can then be rendered on screen to represent different colours, textures and materials. 3D modelling programs such as ProDesktop are widely available.

For example, architects will commission experts to convert their 2D building plans into rendered, 3D, computer-generated 'models'. Once finished, virtual tours can be created which allow the architect and client to travel through the building, viewing it from different angles before a brick has been laid.

Advantages:

- Compared with using an expensive, physical, scale model, virtual modelling provides a more versatile method of communicating a design because it is possible to zoom out in order to view the design in a large environment and zoom in to 'walk' inside the building.
- It is possible to experiment with different materials, colours and textures very easily by using the rendering program. It is even possible to change the lighting conditions to get an impression of the building at different times of day.
- Structural changes can be made very easily and most programs will adjust the rest of the design automatically.
- Many commercial 3D modelling programs allow structural tests to be simulated on the building to ensure safety.
- The work can be used for promotional purposes as it is very easy to understand.

Storage of product and design data

There are many ways of storing data in fixed and portable formats. Large amounts of information can be stored electronically. Examples of electronic storage devices include:

- network servers
- local hard disk
- floppy discs
- CD-ROMs
- other portable devices.

ELECTRONIC COMMUNICATIONS

ICT – through email, the Internet and video conferencing – is used to make sure that all parts of a company are able to communicate and transfer information electronically across the company network. These systems aim to eliminate the need for paperwork and other manual methods of transferring data.

Advantages of using ICT:

- Instant transmissions of documents speeds product development and production process.
- There is no need to print a copy of the document or pay postage so reducing overall costs.
- The technology encourages flexibility in the workforce because people do not have to work in the same office, town or even country.

Email

This is the most common form of communicating electronically from computer to computer.

Advantages of using email:

- Other electronic devices now make email available without the need for a computer.
- Web-based email means that people can retrieve their emails from anywhere in the world.
- Documents or designs can be sent as attachments.
- It is fast, with no loss in accuracy, speeding up the design and manufacturing processes.
- Many programs with a range of features are available which help to organise email, making this a very powerful communication and marketing tool.

The Internet

Advantages of using the Internet:

- Market research information can be gathered from people who visit the website by requiring them to register with the site.
- Companies can use the Internet to find suppliers and potential customers.
- Companies can promote themselves through websites and advertise using a variety of methods.

Video Conferencing

This allows people in different parts of the world to hold virtual meetings. The technology uses digital video cameras and computer networks allowing people to see and hear each other in real time as well as hear each other. Designers, manufacturers and executives can meet to pool resources without leaving their offices.

Advantages:

- It removes the need to travel to meetings, saving time, travel expenses and stress.
- Ease of use enables designers, manufacturers and executives to meet ensuring regular communication, immediate decisions and close control of the development process.
- Education and training can be carried out more efficiently. Expertise can be shared across the company without the need to travel.
- Problems can be solved much more effectively since the relevant experts can meet immediately to address the problem, reducing lost production time.

INDUSTRIAL APPLICATION

Optical Character Recognition (OCR) software is used to 'read' scanned text.

PRODUCTION CONTROL

Many industries use an interlinked network of computers which control almost every aspect of production from design and stock control to quality checks of the finished product. Raw materials and products can be moved automatically without the need for human intervention using an **ASRS** (automatic storage and retrieval system), automatic conveyor systems and **AGVs** (automatic guided vehicles). Engineers ensure that all computers share information and communicate with one another, linking production systems, business information and manufacturing operations. CAD files, for example, can be used to generate costing estimates and orders for raw materials. It is almost possible to control the entire process centrally from one computer terminal.

Advantages of computer-integrated manufacture (CIM)

- Ease of control over complex production system by using integrated ICT network.
- Highly efficient system due to levels of automation and investment in CNC machinery which means products can be produced rapidly.
- Consistently high quality products due to use of CAD/CAM and effective quality control with use of sensors and automatic measuring machines such as CMMs (coordinate measurement machine).
- Requires lower levels of labour reducing operating costs.

Advantages of remote manufacturing

The ability to communicate instantly, using video conferencing, with people all over the world combined with new technologies allowing reliable electronic data exchange means that designs can be manufactured anywhere in the world, that is, remote manufacturing.

- Video conferencing and other communication technologies ensure that designs can be developed in discussion with the manufacturer to ensure they meet the constraints of the manufacturing process.

- The finished design can be sent electronically, directly to the manufacturing centre where it is machined using CNC equipment. The process can be monitored by the design team using video.
- The whole process is very quick and the finished components can be checked and dispatched the same day.
- The process allows designers the opportunity to take advantage of CNC manufacturing technology without having to make the heavy investment necessary to purchase all the machinery.

STOCK CONTROL

Stock control is the process of maintaining appropriate levels of raw materials, components and manufactured products. It costs money to store and manage these, so most companies try to keep levels as low as possible without allowing them to become exhausted by variations in demand. This would be impossible without the use of ICT because the system requires accessible, immediate and accurate information so that materials and components can be ordered or even manufactured just before they are needed, reducing wastage and keeping storage costs to a minimum. ICT also allows the use of ASRS enabling products and materials to be stored and despatched safely and efficiently.

Modern electronic point of sale (EPOS) systems perform a wide range of tasks beyond simply scanning and totalling the price of products. The system uses barcodes, which contain a great deal of information, to keep track of products throughout the supply chain. When a product is sold at the checkout in the supermarket the fact is recorded and used to order replacement goods.

Barcode

Advantages of automated stock control systems:
- Company performance can be monitored at all times due to the availability of detailed and up-to-the-minute records of transactions.
- Detailed sales histories can be used to predict future trends and fluctuations in demand.
- Companies can react quickly to changes in demand because the system will inform them instantly of unpredicted changes in consumer buying patterns.
- Distribution chains can trace the progress of deliveries to ensure efficiency and allowing transferral of products within a company.
- Minimal stock levels can be maintained saving money and resources.

QUALITY CONTROL

Quality control has been covered in detail elsewhere but it is worth emphasising the role ICT can play in ensuring quality throughout the design and manufacturing process. Manual quality control methods are replaced by sophisticated sensors and probes connected to computer systems which monitor quality automatically.

Advantages of ICT in quality control systems:

- Monitoring is continuous and accurate.
- A wide range of probes and sensors can be employed to check all aspects of quality.
- Data collected can be fed directly into the computer system for analysis and reports can be generated immediately.
- The speed and accuracy of the system allows problems to be identified, analysed and corrected early reducing wastage and costs.

ICT AND QUALITY CONTROL IN THE PRINTING INDUSTRY

Automated printing processes make use of a variety of quality checking methods. Visual checks form an important part of the quality control process but accurate testing can only be carried out with the use of sensors and electronic equipment. Quality control checks are carried out on the printed control strip incorporated on the waste areas of the printed sheet. Checking registration marks and colour bars periodically, ensures correct image registration and colour balance. Colour density (thickness) can be measured on the colour bar using a device called a densitometer.

crop marks to show where pages should be trimmed

greyscale

registration marks – to line up four colour separations exactly

Registration marks and control strips

BATCH PRODUCTION OF BUSINESS CARDS

Printing by its very nature is a batch production process. Printing machines produce batches of products ('print runs') ordered by clients and then have to be set immediately for the next order. Larger companies are able to afford larger, faster and more automated printing machines.

In this example, a company has decided to order a large quantity of business cards:

- The designer meets with the client to discuss requirements and a specification is drawn up.
- The client is shown stock examples which are **stored on the computer**.
- To save time the client **emails** a digital version of the company logo.
- A design is developed on the computer using **DTP** software.
- The client approves the design.
- Offset lithography is chosen as the most appropriate printing process.
- The **software is used to reduce the design** to the four-process colours: cyan, magenta, yellow and black (colour separation).
- Individual printing plates are produced for each colour.
- The plates are used to produce a colour proof (some companies possess the technology to produce colour proofs **directly from the computer** at the design stage).
- The client approves the design.
- A full print run then takes place.
- The **computer-controlled printing machine** is set up for the next run.
- An industrial guillotine is used to cut the cards to size.
- The cards are packaged and dispatched to the client.

VOLUME PRODUCTION OF NEWSPAPERS AND MAGAZINES

Regular publications such as newspapers and magazines are subject to strict deadlines. Companies rely heavily on ICT to coordinate the work of the large number of people involved in the production process.

A newspaper company is made up of a large number of departments which are responsible for different parts of the newspaper. A computer network links all these departments to each other. For example:

- a graphic design department creates adverts and special graphics using **draw, paint, photo and desktop publishing software**
- journalists **word process** reports directly into the newspaper computer network or send them electronically
- photographers **scan** their pictures into the network
- classified advertisements are **word processed**
- editors are now able to check and amend all of the material
- **desktop publishing** templates are used to lay out text and images into columns.
- individual copies of the pages, called proofs, are printed to check for mistakes.

Once the design is agreed, the newspaper is produced:

- For each page the **colours are separated electronically** and used to make the lithographic plates which are inserted onto the rollers.
- Huge rolls of newsprint paper are fed into the printing machines.
- A sample proof is printed to check everything has been set up correctly before the run is started.
- From the moment the process starts checks continue, using **automatic sensing equipment** and visual inspections. Possible problems include drifting colour values, poor registration or poor paper quality.
- The printed roll is cut using guillotines, collated and folded.
- Samples are checked visually for quality including correct page order.

Finally, the newspapers are bound and despatched.

Examination questions

 *Explain **two** ways in which ICT can help to improve stock control.*

 4 marks

Acceptable answer

1 **EPOS systems** can be used which will allow the **company to keep accurate track of stocks and sales** throughout the supply chain.
2 Investing in ICT means that **automatic storage and retrieval systems** can be used in warehouses. ASRS can **handle heavy items efficiently and is safer, quicker and more reliable** than using conventional systems.

 *Describe **three** ways in which ICT can be used in the production of business cards.*

 6 marks

Acceptable answer

1 The designer will use **DTP** software to **design the layout** of the card.
2 By **using email** the designer, printer and client can **communicate changes to the design** quickly and efficiently.
3 The **printing machines will be controlled by computer** which can carry out **quality control checks automatically**.

Section 3: Assessment Objective 3

HOW TECHNOLOGY AFFECTS SOCIETY AND OUR OWN LIVES

You need to be aware of:

☐ the development of modern and smart materials

☐ how safety standards organisations and consumer legislation (laws) help to ensure product reliability

☐ the growth of electronic communications and global networks

☐ the use of CAD/CAM to produce products in quantity cheaply.

KEY POINTS

Modern materials are new materials or new combinations of materials which are developed by engineers and scientists.

Smart materials change their properties when subjected to specific conditions. Both present the designer with exciting challenges.

Advantage:

• New materials allow designers to develop new products or to improve existing ones.

Disadvantage:

• Research and development are expensive in the short run.

When we purchase a product or service in the UK, we immediately fall under the protection of a wide range of legislation (laws) and safety organisations. We have a right to expect that manufacturers and advertisers will not mislead us and that their products will not harm us when used in accordance with instructions. We also expect these products to function properly and to be of sufficient quality to last for a reasonable length of time.

The use of CAD/CAM has helped many industries to automate production, which allows more products to be produced in volume with lower costs.

xaminer's Tip

You will only be required to demonstrate an **awareness** of issues in this section (AO3). You will not be required to recall detailed factual information.

MODERN AND SMART MATERIALS

Material	Description	Uses	Advantages
Light sensitive plastics	Plastics which change in response to light	Light reactive spectacles Microprocessors using optical fibre technology	Removes the need to use electronic systems
Thermocolour film (Temperature sensitive coatings)	A liquid which changes colour in response to changes in temperature. It can be put into microscopic capsules which can be printed onto paper or plastic to form a 'heat sensitive film'	Test panels on some batteries Some inexpensive plastic thermometers Warning panels on computer chips to indicate overheating Also available in school kits to form simple displays	An inexpensive and versatile method of indicating temperature changes Requires very little space
Optical fibres	Thin glass fibres which use light to transmit information	Telecommunications cables Mini cameras used in surgery	Light travels much faster through glass fibres when compared with conventional electricity and copper wires. Fibre optics allow more information to be processed much faster than conventional means The technology allows smaller devices to be created
Composite materials	Combining two or more materials that have quite different properties to form new materials	MDF is a composite which consists of wood fibres bonded together using a strong glue Plastic sheeting can be reinforced to resist tearing by combing it with Nylon fibre mesh Kevlar is an extremely strong composite, used in military aircraft and bullet proof vests	The different materials work together to give the composite enhanced and unique properties

BSI

The British Standards Institute is an independent organisation which develops and publishes sets of safety and quality standards for many different areas. It is responsible for establishing tests for products which claim to meet these standards.

Products which meet the appropriate standards can carry the Kitemark but companies need to demonstrate that quality control systems are in place to ensure that products will continue to meet these standards.

Consumers are protected by:

- national and international legislation (laws)
- national and international safety, quality and testing organisations such as the BSI Kitemark.

Kitemark

Advantages:

- Consumers benefit from being able to identify safe and quality products.
- Accurate product information is available to consumers, allowing more informed choice.
- In many areas it is the responsibility of the retailer to ensure quality and safety.
- The consumer is supported by national organisations which exist to enforce legal standards.
- Manufacturers benefit from clearly defined standards.
- Manufacturers benefit from increased sales.

Disadvantage:

- It is more expensive to produce products to exacting standards.

PRODUCT LABELLING

The content of most product labelling is subject to laws which are designed to help the consumer. For example, legislation specifies the information which must be included on food/drink labelling and packaging. Manufacturers who fail to adhere to these regulations are liable to prosecution.

In accordance with this legislation, packaging:

- must describe the product clearly
- must not mislead the customer with false or exaggerated claims.

It must also clearly display:

- the name of the product
- a list of ingredients in descending order of quantity
- a 'best before' date (or 'sell-by' date for perishable food)
- the quantity or weight of product
- the name and address of the manufacturer
- the origin of the product
- storage instructions and conditions of use.

NEW COMMUNICATIONS TECHNOLOGY

The development of new technology – email, mobile telephone networks, the Internet – has enabled us to gather information and communicate more easily.

Advantages of new communications technology:

- instant access to a wealth of information such as stock market prices
- instant access to a range of services such as Internet banking
- instant global communications such as the use of mobile phones and emails.

Disadvantages of new communications technology:

- access to inappropriate material requires the need for filtering software
- spread of computer viruses through email
- increase in unsolicited commercial email – 'spam' – which wastes time and resources
- difficult to control illegal reproduction of material and to enforce copyright law
- access to new technology requires expensive equipment excluding those who cannot afford it.

Many companies use the Internet, not only to promote their products and services, but as a market. Some companies trade exclusively on the Internet.

Advantages of e-commerce:

- There is access to a global market place for relatively small companies.
- All business can be conducted from one geographical site, reducing costs.
- A large part of the transaction process can be automated reducing the need for sales staff.
- Product information is easily accessible and can be changed or updated instantly.
- The use of ICT throughout the process leads to speed and efficiency.

Disadvantages of e-commerce:

- Consumers can feel there is too much advertising on the Internet (e.g. 'pop-up' advertisements).
- Consumers may feel vulnerable to fraud when paying for goods online.

INDUSTRIAL
APPLICATION

Companies such as Amazon.com trade exclusively on the Internet.

Designers have a responsibility to make their work accessible to as many people as possible. For example, it is more cost-effective for an architect to include access for disabled people to a building at the design stage than to add it later. Technology can make it easier for the designer to cater for different needs. For example, when creating an official information leaflet software can be used to translate the document for non-English speakers and text can be enlarged for people who are visually impaired.

USE OF CAD/CAM

The increased reliance on computers has improved manufacturing efficiency and has led to a change in working patterns.

The advantages of CAD/CAM include:

- increased efficiency
- increased flexibility
- reduced unit costs.

The disadvantages include:

- a reduction in the workforce
- increased flexibility and new skills required from the workforce
- large investment required.

Examination questions

 Q1 *Explain the meaning of the term 'smart materials'.*

 2 marks

Acceptable answer

Smart materials **change their properties** when **subjected to specific conditions** such as changes in temperature.

 Q2 *Describe the effects of **two** problems which have become associated with the growth in email communications.*

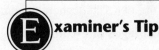 4 marks

Acceptable answer

1 **Viruses have been developed** which spread through the email network. They have **slowed down global networks**/have been designed to **cause damage to computer files**.

2 There has been a **big increase in the use of unsolicited commercial email** (spam). **This wastes time and resources/promotes inappropriate material**.

Examiner's Tip

Remember to expand explanations beyond your initial point.

IMPACT OF VALUES AND ISSUES ON DESIGN AND MANUFACTURE

TOPICS

You need to be aware of:

☐ the existence of moral debates

☐ environmental issues

☐ the impact of cultural issues on design for manufacture.

KEY POINTS

By now, you should be aware of the advantages of living in a technology driven society. There are many groups, however, who question aspects of technological progress. Progress has negative as well as positive effects.

Moral issues are arguments over 'right' and 'wrong'. Some laws protect us but many decisions are left for individuals to make. For example, some people would question whether it is morally right to manufacture and advertise toy weapons for children.

The moral debates you need to be aware of are:
- changing fashions
- planned product obsolescence.

You need to be aware of environmental issues:
- sustainable technology
- how resources can be conserved and waste reduced by **reducing** packaging materials, **recycling** and by encouraging the **re-use** of packaging products
- pollution produced from PVC packaging.

You also need to be aware of cultural issues:
- the impact of Far Eastern and Japanese culture on design for manufacture.

CHANGING FASHIONS

Fashion has always been an important market force. Consumers switch their product allegiances due to changes in fashion trends. Manufacturers have to be aware of trends and fashions which will affect the demand for their products. Some argue that manufacturers manipulate the market to create demand for products through marketing and advertising. This encourages consumers to buy things which they do not need. Often these companies operate globally and have been accused of behaving unethically in poorer countries.

Arguments for:
- Changing fashion is a natural phenomenon and consumers enjoy spending money on the 'latest fashion'.
- Changing fashions stimulate progress as manufacturers seek to develop and improve their products.

Impact of values and issues on design and manufacture

Arguments against:
- Replacing products based on fashions and trends is a wasteful process and places additional pressures on raw materials and the environment through increased industrial activity.
- Expensive advertising campaigns designed to create demand add a disproportionate amount of money to the price of a product.
- The youth market is particularly vulnerable and is targeted by manufacturers placing undue pressure on families to buy the 'latest thing'.
- Products are marketed unethically in poorer countries where consumers are less informed and do not enjoy the same legal protection from unscrupulous manufacturers and advertisers.

Companies spend a lot of money persuading us to buy their products. Some products such as Coca-Cola or Nike are known all over the world and their logos would be instantly recognised by most people. These companies and their products have a very strong 'brand identity'. These goods tend to be more expensive but people still want to buy them because they want to be associated with the brand.

PLANNED PRODUCT OBSOLESCENCE

Products are designed to last for a certain length of time. The decision is made by the manufacturer, based upon market research. It is not necessary to design mobile phones or computers to last for more than a few years because the consumer tends to upgrade regularly as fashions change or as improvements in technology are made. Point-of-sale displays enjoy an even shorter lifespan and are discarded after the promotion has finished. However, some people feel that certain products should last longer and that manufacturers are designing products with a short lifespan in order to fuel demand. It is argued that this is unnecessarily wasteful and products could be designed for a much longer, useful life.

Arguments for:
- Advances in technology make products obsolete, naturally.
- Changes in fashions and demand create a demand to replace products.
- Products can be cheaper because they do not have to last beyond their nominal lifespan.

Arguments against:
- Products wear out before they need to and could be made to last much longer saving the consumer money in the long run.
- It is a wasteful process and places additional pressures on raw materials and the environment through increased industrial activity.

SUSTAINABLE TECHNOLOGY

Environmental issues are gaining much attention as people fear that the world's resources cannot support the ever-increasing demands of a modern industrialised society. Resources are classified into two groups:
- **renewable** – raw materials which can be replaced, such as replanted trees in managed forests to create paper and boards
- **non-renewable** – raw materials which, once exhausted, cannot be replaced, such as crude oil used to make plastics.

The world's resources may seem plentiful but some people believe that a number of raw materials are beginning to run out and that the by-products of industry are having an irreversible effect upon the environment. Sustainable technology ensures that technological progress does not deplete the world of resources or harm the environment. For example:

- some packaging can be recycled (codes are now moulded into plastic products to aid identification)
- replacing non-renewable resources with renewable resources – solar, hydro and wind power can be used to replace power produced from burning fossil fuels
- ensuring renewable resources are replaced, e.g. replacing trees in managed forests.

INFLUENCE OF FAR EAST AND JAPAN

Culture is the way in which groups of people live. 'Youth culture', for example, has inspired the production of many products. Designers take their inspiration from many different sources. Many look abroad, at other cultures, in order to gain fresh, original ideas. For example, the Far East and Japan have had an influence on design and manufacture:

- **Architectural influences.** Buddhism is an important religion in the Far East. It places an emphasis on simplicity and a close relationship with nature. This is reflected in Japanese architecture where traditional houses are kept very simple, using natural materials and opening out onto carefully designed gardens. Many western designers and architects have borrowed from these styles.
- **Artistic influences.** Products such as the Manga cartoons have inspired western designers to produce graphic work using similar styles.

Manga cartoon

The Far East and Japanese culture have also had an impact on manufacture. For example, modern factory organisation owes a large debt to the Far East where companies have been able to create large, effective, disciplined and motivated workforces. Many of the systems retain their Japanese names such as 'poka-yoke' – the process of simplifying work wherever possible by using foolproof tools, jigs and fixtures.

CONSERVATION OF RESOURCES AND WASTE MANAGEMENT

Reduce

A lot of packaging sometimes seems unnecessary. Designers can help the environment and reduce costs by using as little packaging as possible. The walls of an aluminium can are only 0.1 mm thick and the strength of the unopened can is derived from the pressure of the drink it contains.

Recycle

Many materials can be recycled. However, recycling uses resources and can produce harmful by-products.

Re-use

Consumers can be encouraged to reuse packaging. For example, fabric conditioner is now sold in refill packs which can be poured into the original container and are sold at a lower price.

Recycling symbol

PVC USED IN PACKAGING

Plastics in general have a poor environmental image because they are not biodegradable (do not decompose) or because they pollute the atmosphere when incinerated. PVC, in particular, has been singled out because harmful substances (hydrochloric acid) can be released when it is incinerated. As a result, the use of PVC is controlled in some countries.

However, PVC requires less energy to manufacture than alternatives and is composed largely from chlorine, which is derived from salt which is a plentiful resource. It is also possible to remove harmful substances when PVC is incinerated to prevent them from entering the environment.

Some people believe that paper should be used for grocery bags instead of plastics such as polythene, because paper is better for the environment. However, more energy is required and more pollution is created in the production of paper bags compared with producing the plastic alternative. In addition, consumers are more likely to reuse plastic bags.

Examination questions

 Q1 *Many manufacturers incorporate 'planned product obsolescence' into their goods.*

  a *Give the meaning of 'planned product obsolescence'.*

  b *Describe **one** advantage to the consumer of 'planned product obsolescence'.*

  c *Describe **one** disadvantage to the consumer of 'planned product obsolescence'.*

5 marks

Acceptable answer

a Products are designed to wear out after a set length of time determined by the manufacturer.

b **Products can be cheaper** because **less durable materials and components** are used which decreases the cost of production.

c The consumer has to **replace products more regularly** which usually means **spending more money in the long run**.

 Q2 *Designers and manufacturers have become increasingly aware of their responsibility to the environment. Many have tried to help by minimising the waste produced by packaging. Use the headings below to describe **two** ways in which the use of the illustrated packaging helps the environment.*

4 marks

Bottle

Refill pack

Recycling symbols

Acceptable answer

a Re-using product: The **refill pack can be emptied into the original container**. This refill pack **uses less material and allows the original container to be reused**.

b Recycling materials: The **recycling symbols** on the plastic packaging helps the consumer and recycling centre to **sort waste correctly for recycling**.

Section 4: Advice on design and product analysis questions

This section contains advice on how to answer:

- design questions (not short course)
- product analysis questions.

KEY POINTS

- The design questions on the foundation tier and higher tier will be different.
- The product analysis question for the full course paper will be the same on both foundation and higher tiers. It will appear as question 4 at foundation and question 1 at the higher level.
- The product analysis question for the short course paper will be the same on both foundation and higher tiers. It will appear as question 3 at foundation and question 1 at the higher level.
- Both the design question and the product analysis question will be divided into smaller part questions which use the same key words as listed in Section 1. The type of answers required also follow the same pattern as the examples given in Section 1.
- The way in which these two questions differ from others on the paper is that each will focus completely on a single product, that is, all 22 marks.
- The products used for each question will be different and will be introduced at the beginning of the question.
- Both questions will test your ability to apply knowledge and understanding of the Specification content to the identified product.

DESIGN QUESTIONS

- The design question will test your ability to produce two different, relevant and viable initial designs from a given specification. You must apply your knowledge and understanding gained from studying the following topics of Design and Technology: Graphic Products to the production of your designs.

  (a) Selection of materials and components:
    - material form and intended manufacturing process;
    - functional properties of materials;
    - choice and fitness for purpose of materials and components.

  (b) Processing and finishing materials:
    - combination/processing of materials to create more useful properties;
    - functional properties of finishes – physical and visual.

  (c) Manufacturing commercial products:
    - manufacturing processes suited to the specified production volume.

  (d) Design and market influence:
    - environmental, moral and safety issues relating to material selection;
    - ease of manufacture of your design.

The following bullet points show the type of information given in each design question, supported by examples of wording. Each example is accompanied by brief explanations to help you identify the important things to consider and include in an answer. An example of a full design question with a model answer is included at the end of this section.

Each design question includes the following:

- A brief description of the background to the design situation, for example:

    'A toothbrush manufacturer requires a new design of display packaging for individual toothbrushes.'

- A list of specification points that your design ideas must satisfy. Each of these points will contain two linked elements, both of which must be satisfied in each of your designs to score full marks. An example of one specification point is:

    'Hold a single toothbrush hygienically.'

- The two linked elements to be included in your design are: *'Hold a single toothbrush'* and *'hygienically'*.

- The instructions and marks available for each part of the question, for example:

 Q1 *In the spaces below use notes and sketches to show **two** different designs of your product which meet the specification above.* **(2 × 8 marks)**

---

 xaminer's Tip

You must look at the functional requirements of each specification point and present different methods by which those requirements are met in each of your two separate design ideas.

---

 xaminer's Tip

Remember, there can be many answers that all apear to be different for this type of question. However, all successful answers must satisfy the common specification points given in the question.

---

xaminer's Tip

In part **(a)** of the question, you should produce two different ideas to access both sets of 8 marks. This means your ideas must be technically different, not cosmetically different – that is, a different technical method by which the set design task is satisfied rather than just changing the colour or the shape. For example, printed information can be achieved in technically different ways, that is:
- printed directly onto the packaging material
- printed onto a separate label which is then attached to the package.

Key words

'Use notes and sketches': your answer to the design question should be sketched and supported with notes that clarify the sketches by providing additional important information that cannot easily be shown by sketching.

The 2D element of your design solution should be indicated by annotation only.

 *Three of the specification points are given below. Use these headings to evaluate **one** of your design ideas against the initial specification.* **(6 marks)**

xaminer's Tip

Remember the key word 'evaluate'. This means that one or two sentences are required where the suitability or value of your idea is judged. It can include both positive and negative points, with each point being linked to a feature of your design and being supported with a valid justification or reasoning.

xaminer's Tip

The evaluation you carry out here should result in your giving the examiner new/additional information relating to how well your design is likely to succeed or why it might fail. This new information will be contained in these judgements and their justification or reasoning. It will probably be in the form of an *explanation*; simply repeating information previously *described* in part **(a)** of your answer will not score marks here.

xaminer's Tip

Remember to divide the time you spend on this question in proportion to the marks available for each part, that is:
(a) design idea 1 **(8 marks)** – approximately 8 minutes
(b) design idea 2 **(8 marks)** – approximately 8 minutes
(c) evaluation **(6 marks)** – approximately 6 minutes.

Example design question

A toothbrush manufacturer requires a new design of display packaging for individual toothbrushes.

The specification is that:
- *the packaging must hold a single brush hygienically*
- *the materials selected must allow the consumer to see the product clearly*
- *the packaging must be easily suitable for volume (mass) production*
- *the packaging must display the company logo in a prominent position.*

*In the spaces below use notes and sketches to show **two** ideas for the design of the product which meets this specification.* **(2 × 8 marks)**

Choose one of your design ideas and evaluate it against the three initial design specification points given below.

The packaging must hold a single brush hygienically.
The materials selected must allow the consumer to see the product clearly.
The packaging must be easily suitable for volume (mass) production. **(6 marks)**

Model answer

DESIGN IDEA 1   DESIGN IDEA 2

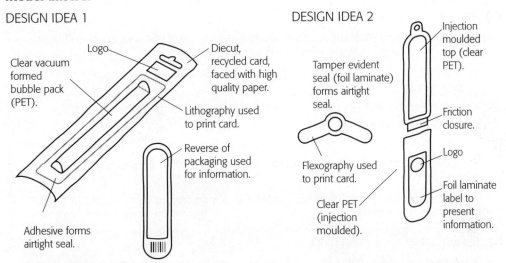

DESIGN IDEA 2

The package consists of a **two-part container** that **encloses the toothbrush completely**. The PET and foil laminate have been chosen because when combined, they **form a good barrier to gases** which will **protect the product from germs**. The foil laminate forms a tamper-evident seal which shows when the **packaging has been opened** as it **needs to be broken to access the product.**

Injection moulded **PET has been chosen because of its glass-like transparency** which allows the customer to **see the product clearly from all sides.**

Because **PET is a thermoplastic** it can be mass produced easily, using **automated injection moulding processes**. The foil laminate selected for the tamper-evident seals and labels can be produced using flexography and die cutting. These can be **highly automated** which make them **fast and inexpensive** processes, suitable for mass production.

PRODUCT ANALYSIS QUESTIONS

Each product analysis question will give information about a commercially produced product in the form of:

- an illustration
- any additional data necessary for you to answer all part questions.

You will then be required to interpret this information and combine it with the knowledge and experience gained from studying Design and Technology: Graphic Products to answer the part questions set from any of the following topics:

(a) Selection of materials and components:

- the working characteristics of materials in relation to their function within the product;
- the relationship of the material's final form in the product and the manufacturing process;
- functional properties of materials in relation to their use in the product;
- choice and fitness for purpose within the product of materials and components.

(b) Processing and finishing materials:

- combination or processing of materials to create more useful properties and how these have been used beneficially within the product;
- functional properties of finishes – physical and visual – and why they are important to the product;
- how the materials have been prepared for the manufacture of the product;
- how and why pre-manufactured standard components have been used in the product;
- where and/or why specified tolerances have been used in the manufacture of the product;
- how and/or why ICT have been used in the design and/or manufacture of the product.

(c) Manufacturing commercial products:

- an awareness of a manufacturing process suited to the specified production volume for the product and an understanding of why it is suitable;
- an awareness of how ICT, including CAD/CAM, is used in batch or volume manufacture of the product.

(d) Design and market influence:

- evaluate the quality of design and quality of manufacture in terms of the product performance criteria related to the following – function, the needs and values of users, moral, cultural and environmental considerations, the materials and processes used, safety and value for money;
- consider the design features that make the product suitable for manufacture in the specified quantity;
- planning of production for the product including production schedules, quality control and quality assurance.

(e) Give and justify points of specification for the given product.

xaminer's Tip

Remember, not all of these topics will be covered each year and just because a topic was covered in a previous year does not mean that it will not be included again.

Example questions
The following are examples of part question types that may be included in product analysis questions. Each part question is linked to the product described in the introduction.

xaminer's Tip

Key words
Remember, the type and complexity of answers required to any part question is shown by the use of the key words used in the question, that is, Give, State, Name, Describe, Explain, etc.

For this example, the question would start by showing an illustration of a point-of-sale display made from solid board and labelled to show where graphics are to be applied and where tabs are to be glued.

Q3 *Two points of specification for the point-of-sale display are:*
- *it must hold 24 chocolate bars securely;*
- *it must attract potential customers.*

Give **three** *more points which must be included in the specification for the point-of-sale display. For each point give a reason why it must be included.*

1 ....

Reason ....

2 ....

Reason ....

3 ....

Reason .... **(6 marks)**

A full answer for 6 marks requires three valid points of specification for the product, each linked with a valid reason for its inclusion, for example:

1 It must incorporate the **product logo** because of the need to **promote brand/ product recognition**.
2 It must be **lightweight** because of the **need to move it easily** in a changing shop display.

3 It must be **robust and durable** because it must **retain a good appearance for an acceptable period of time**.

xaminer's Tip

Note that each of the answers is given in two parts – the point of specification followed by the reason. The two parts are linked by the word 'because'.

Another key word may be used in this question – 'Complete'. For example:

 The design for the point-of-sale display is to be made as a one-off prototype using manual cut and paste techniques.

Complete the block diagram below to show, in the correct sequence, **four** more main stages in making the point-of-sale display as a one-off prototype.

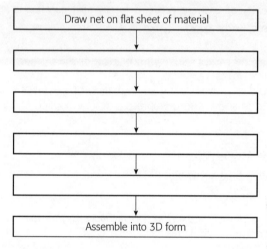

Draw net on flat sheet of material

Assemble into 3D form

(5 marks)

A full answer for 5 marks requires four main stages to be written in the spaces provided, and in the correct sequence, for example four from: add graphics while flat; cut around net shape to remove waste; score all fold lines; pre-fold all fold lines; apply glue to glue tabs. You would receive 4 marks for the main stages and 1 mark for the correct sequence.

xaminer's Tip

Note that the wording of each stage in the question is a brief phrase. This is a guide to show the detail required in the answers; each stage of the answer given above is a brief phrase – single-word answers will seldom give enough information to fully identify an individual stage and earn the mark.